THE BEAUTY
OF THE BEASTS

THE BEAUTY
OF THE BEASTS

Tales of Hollywood's Wild Animal Stars

RALPH HELFER

JEREMY P. TARCHER, INC.
Los Angeles

Library of Congress Cataloging in Publication Data

Helfer, Ralph.
    The beauty of the beasts: tales of Hollywood's wild animal stars/Ralph Helfer.
        p. cm.
    1. Animals in motion pictures.   2. Motion pictures—California—Los Angeles.
    3. Captive wild animals.   I. Title.   II. Title: Hollywood's wild animal stars.
    PN1995.9.A5H45   1990
    791.43′66—dc20   89-20383
    ISBN 0-87477-516-7   CIP

Jeremy P. Tarcher, Inc.
5858 Wilshire Blvd., Suite 200
Los Angeles, CA 90036

Distributed by St. Martin's Press, New York

Design by Tanya Maiboroda

Manufactured in the United States of America

10 9 8 7 6 5 4 3 2 1

First Edition

To Tana, my inspiration;
Toni, who shared Camelot;
Cathi, for believing in me;
and
Zamba, my mentor

CONTENTS

CONTENTS

Part III
"NO PROBLEM"

Part IV
GIMMICKS AND GADGETS

Part V
HOLLYWOOD'S WILD LIFE

ACKNOWLEDGMENTS

No one can do it alone. Throughout my life I have been indebted to various people along the way, people who were there for me at the right time and place. Such a person entered my life when this book was just a title. She has been there through the rough period when the words just didn't come out right. She has had the compassion, warmth, patience, and understanding to stick by my side until the very end. For this I will be eternally grateful. My love and thanks to Laurie Rose.

In addition, I would like to express my gratitude to the following individuals:

For his dedication and for creating the opportunity for me to share my stories, I would like to thank my publisher, Jeremy Tarcher.

For his help in the early stages of editing the book, my appreciation goes to Hank Stine.

For her affection training of me as a writer, my appreciation goes to Stephanie Eve Bernstein, my editor.

PROLOGUE

On one of my many visits to Africa, I spent an afternoon visiting with one of the world's foremost exporters of wild animals. With my lion Rafiki (which is Swahili for "friend") half asleep at my feet, we sat on a veranda sipping sundowners, watching a flock of marabou storks settling into the nearby yellow fever trees at the foot of Kilimanjaro.

But in spite of the peaceful vistas in front of us, the atmosphere on the porch was tense. I had just won a six-figure contract to supply a full-grown African lion for an upcoming film. At that time I had the only animals in the world who were qualified to perform the full range of actions required by this particular script.

My host had lost the contract due to his method of training—a method that was widespread in the industry at the time. Like many other trainers, he firmly believed that lions had to be worked with a strong hand, which meant that the constant threat of physical abuse was used to dominate the animal. While this method was effective for many animal acts, it was not safe when physical contact between an animal and a performer was involved. Whenever a movie scene called for a hands-on approach with a mature lion, for example, directors were forced to use one of several options. For some scenes, a mechanical lion could be built, allowing the actors to work closely with the "animal" without danger. For attack scenes, a young animal—sometimes wearing a fake mane—could be substituted. Or, in moments of desperation, a taxidermied animal could be thrown or launched at the actor, who would fall to the ground, stabbing the dummy until the stuffing flew out and the director yelled, "Cut!" (In such scenes, the greatest danger was that of being knocked out by the hurtling stuffed animal!)

Before the studio located my lion, in fact, they had been having a replica of a lion built in Germany for the scenes in which the use of a live animal would endanger the actor. Once they found my uniquely trained lion, they stopped building the replica, since everything could now be filmed using a live, mature lion.

My host was eager to know what techniques I was using to control my animal. He assumed that I was using some type of drug that made the animal tractable. He was suspicious of my animals, and he was equally suspicious of me. Being of the old school, he believed that the more scars one had, the more marks of distinction one had earned as a trainer.

"Look at Joe," he said, beckoning his chief trainer to come over to where we were sitting. He grabbed Joe's right arm. "Two fingers missing to a tough old leopard. And how about this one?" he continued, rolling up his own pant leg. A deep scar ran from his knee back to the middle of his calf. "This lion damn near killed me!" he bragged. "What about you, Ralph? What do you have to show for it?"

I shrugged, unwilling to enter that competition. It was true that in the beginning of my career as a stuntman and wild-animal trainer, I had been clawed by lions, attacked by bears, bitten by poisonous snakes, and nearly suffocated by pythons. But that had been when I was handling animals the same way that he did.

"Since I discovered affection training, I have nothing to show," I said. "Not a scratch."

My host snorted in disbelief. "Affection *what?*"

I wasn't exactly surprised by his reaction; my peers in the States had been equally hostile.

"Affection training. Instead of dealing with my animals physically, I deal with them emotionally. I know this is going to sound crazy to you, but I use love, patience, understanding, and respect to get my animals to perform."

My host and his trainer exchanged smug looks. Just then, the maid brought us out a dinner tray of steak sandwiches and drinks. At the smell of food, Rafiki stretched, yawned, and rose to his feet. Without being conscious of it, my host drew his injured leg in closer to him, away from the lion. The topic shifted to the poaching problems plaguing Africa.

Midway through the meal I casually slipped a thick piece of rare steak to Rafiki, who carefully took it from my hand and then lay down to savor it.

The entire scene was not lost on my host, who was amazed by Rafiki's eating cooked meat, as well as by his gentleness. He knew that he could never do that with any of his own lions.

At sunset I loaded Rafiki into the backseat of the Land Rover and we took off, with the lion's majestic head sticking up through the open sunroof.

On the ride back to our location site I reflected on the meeting. I knew my host had been impressed, not with what I had said, but with what he had seen. Perhaps he wouldn't change his way of training animals, but others surely would.

In the years to follow, my affection-training approach to working with animals revolutionized the way in which wild animals could be handled. The old method of fear training was not humane, and animals trained this way were dangerous to work with. In contrast, affection training is highly humane and extremely safe. Performances that would previously have been impossible were now regular occurrences, and the possibilities were limited only by the imagination.

For the first time, a person could handle full-grown bears and leopards safely, a child could ride on a tiger's back, and a lion could really lie down with a lamb! In many ways, the "peaceable kingdom" had become a reality.

PART I

THE TURNING POINT

I *never envisioned myself as a pioneer.*

Ever since I was a boy, I'd known that I would spend my life immersed in the world of animals. To me, the animal kingdom was more perfect than the human one.

I became a professional stuntman and wild-animal trainer so that I could combine my passion for animals with my love of the silver screen. I was quickly disillusioned. The approach used to train animals for films went against my belief that fear should not be used to make an animal perform. Even though I had no animals of my own then, I was required to use this technique with the animals I was hired to work with. I found the experience very distressing.

Most people follow the teachings of those who came before them, whether they believe these teachings are right or wrong. After a brush with death, I no longer had the choice to blindly follow where others had led me. I had to create something new, to pioneer a new approach. Intuitively, I knew that there must be a way to train animals so that they would enjoy performing as much as the viewing public enjoyed watching them. Only then could my life be centered around the beauty of the beasts.

1

BWANA SIMBA

The grass was damp from the early-morning dew as we sat on a small hillock against a majestic old acacia tree. Zamba, my lion, lay Sphinxlike beside me, scanning the African plain 1,000 feet below. Pam, a mere pixie of a child actress, sat close, nestled against my shoulder. One of my companions was huge and powerful; the other, innocent and trusting.

A warm breeze blew across the ridge; the silence was broken only by the lion's heavy breathing.

It was time.

I got up and dusted off my jeans, and we headed up the slope. Zamba walked between Pam and me, with Pam's hand resting gently on his thick, golden mane. She could barely see over his back.

We stopped under the swaying arches of a giant yellow fever tree. Just ahead were the camera and crew, quietly waiting to film, for the first time ever, a 68-pound, nine-year old child wrestling a full-grown, 528-pound lion. I knelt down beside Pam, and our eyes met.

"Pam, you must remember the things I've taught you, especially that Zamba is very strong and that you must never get under him, since his weight is too much for you."

Pam's eyes twinkled, and she broke into a smile.

"Don't worry, we'll do just fine."

I stood up, ruffled Pam's hair, and we headed toward the shooting location.

Suddenly, I felt a hand on my shoulder, and I turned. Pam's mother was there.

"Mom!" Pam gave her a hug. "What are you doing here? I thought you had to wait for us down below."

There was an embarrassed silence.

"I know I shouldn't be here, Ralph," Mrs. Franklin blurted out to me, hugging Pam to her. "But Pam is my daughter. My *only* daughter." I could see a bit of fright edging across the corner of her lip. She continued, "And I love her dearly."

"Oh, Mommy, nothing's going to happen to me," Pam said in her lilting English accent. She looked up at me, her Peter Pan haircut accentuating her large brown eyes. Her whole face seemed to say, "I trust you."

"I'm not questioning your judgment, Ralph, but I'm just a little scared for her," Mrs. Franklin said. "This is the first time Pam will be working alone with Zamba."

"Mom," Pam protested, "I've been training with Zamba for three months! He wouldn't hurt me. That's just silly." She put her hands on her hips. "Zamba loves me! And I love him! I love all animals—you know that, *Bwana Simba!*"

I smiled. It was the first time she'd called me that. "Where did you hear 'Bwana Simba'?" I asked her.

"The Africans told me that anybody who can handle lions like you do should be called that."

I gave Pam's shoulder a little squeeze, then turned to her mother. "Look, Mrs. Franklin, I feel about Pam the way that I would about my own daughter. There's no way I would put her in any sort of jeopardy."

There was a deep sigh. Pam's mother took her daughter's hand, and then mine. She was trembling. "Okay, *Bwana*. I'll wait for you both down below."

She gave Pam a hug and headed back down the slope.

Zamba was getting restless, so we continued on to the site.

The view from the top was fantastic—one could see for miles in all directions. I settled Zamba down onto the soft grassy area where the scene was going to take place.

Bill Holden was the star of the movie. He sat with his back against an acacia tree. As I shot a look in his direction, he smiled an "I'm with you" smile. The crew, however, seemed unusually quiet. They were huddled in small, murmuring groups, their voices kept at a whisper. It set the tone of a funeral. I wanted to scream, "It's okay!! Zamba won't hurt her, he *loves* her!"

I motioned Pam to take her place at Zamba's side. The scene needed to look like two innocent children at play—rolling over and over, one on top, then the other, pulling hair, mane, holding hands, paws.

A lion's favorite prey are the young. The high-pitched voices and quick, fragile movements excite them. Only Zamba's love for the little girl would keep him from harming her.

Zamba turned his great head. His enormous eyes settled on Pam, looking at her, through her—and then he turned away to focus on the animals far off on the veldt.

"Are you ready, honey?" asked the director.

"Yes," came Pam's small voice.

What was I doing? Can a man have this much faith in a lion? Trainers the world over had turned the job down, saying it was impossible, that no adult lion could work safely with a child. I knew otherwise. So did Pam. We knew!

She's my only daughter. . . . The words kept coming back to me.

I positioned Pam on her side, lying beside Zamba. He looked down at her, giving a low, throaty sound, similar to those that lionesses make to their cubs.

"Okay, Pam?" I asked.

"Okay, Bwana." She smiled.

I touched Zamba's foot as a reminder to him to keep his claws sheathed. Then I put my finger on his wet nose. "Stay!" I said, and backed away to a spot near the camera. A voice rang out, "Roll camera! Action!"

Pam started to talk to Zamba.

"Hi, big boy. How's my baby? You want to play?" Zamba responded. He sat up. Pam lay below him. *Don't get under him,* I said to myself. *Easy, Zamba.*

Zamba looked down at her like a cat looking down at a mouse. Then he moved.

One big mass of hair, muscle, and tawniness encircled Pam. He gathered her little body up and scooped her to him. She was a leaf caught in the wind. Her frail arms stretched out, as if to hold a teddy bear.

Zamba's eyes became intense. Pam's head was directly below his jaws. Then a cold shiver ran through my whole body as I saw Zamba reach down with his mouth and bury his huge head into her neck!

Like a steel spring, I shot straight up, a thousand horrors racing through my mind.

Then I heard it. A giggle . . . then another, like water tumbling down a brook. Zamba was licking Pam's neck, and his tongue was tickling her. My God, what a relief! What ecstasy! I settled down, and for the next few minutes we all watched the little girl and big lion "wrestle."

Zamba engulfed Pam in his paws. She tickled him and, rolling over on top, buried her head in his thick mane. They were like two rough-and-tumble kids. After what seemed like an eternity, the director yelled, "Cut!" and the crew burst into applause. A few tears appeared and were quickly brushed away.

Bill threw his arms around me. "Ralph, you did it!"

"Weren't they great?"

Zamba and I left the set and headed for the coolness of the yellow fever trees to await the next setup. We were alone . . . together. I stretched out in the forest's thickness. Zamba lay his head across my lap, and I stroked his red-gold mane.

I closed my eyes and savored the moment. How proud I was of both of them—Pam, for trusting and believing in me, and Zamba, for showing the world that affection training works.

We had come a long way.

✳

"CUT! CUT!!" screamed the director. "Good God! Somebody *help* him!"

Too late! There were two huge, gaping fang holes in my arm, big enough that I could see the studio ceiling arc lights shining through. The pain was excruciating. This lion was BIG—a good 500 pounds. He was hovering inches above me now, one foot on my chest, roaring and snarling in rage.

Helpless, I was lying on the floor of the steel-barred arena, with the hot light pouring down. Amidst the sweat, blood, and terror, I promised myself that if I made it out of this one, I would never work with another animal that had been trained with fear. Outside the arena I could hear people screaming, yelling, rushing everywhere. One man opened the arena door and hurled the director's chair at the lion to try to get him off me. A woman stood at the bars shouting to the lion to let me go.

Why should he? I had teased and humiliated him with a whip and chair, which now lay ten feet away, and he was *mad!*

Anyway, I was dead, or about to be.

But I didn't want to die and have people say, "Well, he *should* have died! Just look what he was doing to that lion, using a *whip!*"

I froze. Those eyes, those huge, amber eyes, had gone blood red.

He bit me again, somewhere. I felt my flesh pop open. Things were vague . . . blurred. My brain was numb. Then I couldn't see—there was blood in my eyes! The lion snarled, and I caught a glimpse of a white fang streaked with blood.

I heard the clanking of a steel door and the rattling of the bars. Somebody was coming! I felt an ice-cold blast. A fire extinguisher! The CO_2 hit the lion in the face. My rescuer was a very brave man, I thought. Then the great weight of the lion was gone.

Hands were grabbing me, pulling me across the floor. I felt myself being shoved through a door.

Sounds of steel, then of someone yelling, "CLOSE THAT GODDAMN DOOR!!" Someone else shouted, "SOME-BODY! QUICK! QUICK!!"

Slam! Slam! Slam! They were echoes of safety.

"Will everyone please evacuate the arena area!" boomed a voice over the loudspeaker.

A man yelled, "call an ambulance!!!"

❋

I awoke to the sun's brilliance lighting up my hospital room early the next morning. I felt terrified. I seemed to remember that the doctor had amputated my arm the night before. Frantically, I grabbed for the stump—but no, my arm was still there! Whole, but very painful. I must have dreamt it, a nightmare coming from the pain and anguish of the attack.

It was still very early, and the room was quiet. My mind shot back to that horrible moment when I had felt the lion's hot breath on my cheek. The lion had meant to kill me! The attack epitomized what happens when an animal is fear trained. This lion was distrustful of humans, even vengeful toward them.

Never again, I told myself, my mind fighting against the drugs as I lapsed in and out of consciousness. There had to be a better way to work with animals.

Then sleep overtook me. Suddenly I was a kid, alone in an alley in my old Chicago neighborhood. It was pitch-dark, and deafeningly still. I began to run, tripping on the fractured asphalt that jutted upward. The stench of refuse was everywhere, spilling out from the overturned garbage cans. Rats—some of them as big as cats—were fighting over the garbage. They streaked past in all directions, shrieking and clawing their way across my feet. Then, up ahead, I could see something shimmering—a forest, gleaming like an emerald in the distance. Every agonizing step brought me closer, closer. . . .

Finally, I burst into the center of a clearing. Crystalline beads of dew sparkled on every leaf in the bright sunlight. The meadow was filled with animals—tigers, elephants, lions, goats, horses, and lambs—all lying peacefully beside one another.

Then, as though called by a piper, they began to drift away. I felt devastated and cried out to them, "Don't go! Don't leave me!"

I awoke, bathed in sweat. A nurse was mopping my brow. After she left, I kept thinking about the dream. Ever since early childhood, I wanted to be able to know an animal's world and to let it know mine. True, as a wild-animal trainer, my life did revolve around animals, but the basis of my relationship with them was fear. All the training books, magazines, and films espoused the fear-training method: "Use a

whip, a gun, and a chair." "Animals only understand dominance." "Survival of the fittest." "Force the animal to submit."
"Put fear in them, to the point of causing physical pain." *No
wonder the lion tried to kill me!*

True, I had learned from the best. But what the "best" had to
teach was not what I had wanted. I wasn't interested in domi-
nation; I was interested in communication. I realized that fear
training went against everything I believed in. I was a *lover* of
nature. My dream said it all: the lion and the lamb.

Could it be possible to work with animals without using
fear-training methods? Could an animal be trained with love
alone? I doubted it—after all, children raised that way turn out
spoiled. No, there had to be more to the training: the *love* needed
to be tempered by *understanding*. The animal needed to be known
so well that its every move could be anticipated and dovetailed
with the needs of the trainer.

But such a depth of understanding could hardly be gained
overnight. It would take months, years of work. It would require
extraordinary, even superhuman, patience. But I didn't care *how*
long it took. If it took forever, it would be worth it to undo
centuries of physical abuse.

But would love, understanding, and patience actually be
enough? If the lion that had attacked me in the arena had been
loved, understood, and treated with patience, he *still* might
have attacked me. What was missing was *respect:* mine for him,
and his for me. Achieving dominance by bullying and causing
fear and pain was no way to create a mutually respectful relationship. But to achieve an animal's cooperation through true
respect—now *that* would be an achievement worth devoting
one's life to.

A new approach to working with wild animals was slowly
taking form in my mind. Dominating the animals physically
was out of the question, since they're so much more powerful
than we are. I also had to rule out working with them on an
intellectual plane, since they're just not on the same level as
we are.

But to work with them by using emotions—*that* was a real

possibility. In the realm of emotions, animals and humans share a common ground.

Affection training was born.

✱

After leaving the hospital, I restructured my thinking, and my company. I let go of those trainers whose past experience in training animals had involved fear techniques, and in their place I hired not other trainers, but animal lovers.

How excited we all were! Was it possible? Could it really work? I was determined to find out.

PART II

THE EARLY
DAYS

Looking back, I can see that the early days of struggle were some of the best. Although we suffered from the elements, food was sparse, and money was hard to come by, we were inspired by our vision of what our future with wild animals could become. The warmth and enjoyment we received from our animals more than compensated us for any hardships we endured.

These were the days of proving myself. Would my theory work in practice?

At first I was criticized, harassed, even denounced. I was told I was "wasting time," "spending hard-earned money," or "going down the wrong track." But the critics were wrong. Affection training did work. In fact, it worked so well that when people saw how calm my animals were, they claimed I had drugged them!

I built my stock up slowly, always trying to get animals when they were very young—even before their eyes had opened—so that we would be imprinted as their surrogate parents. In the meantime, I often had to work with fear- or reward-trained animals, which were sometimes unpredictable or even dangerous.

Despite the uphill battle I faced among the professional community, the reputation of my animals gradually began to make its way through the entertainment industry. My affection-trained animals allowed me to progress as a stuntman, enabling me to work with adult lions, tigers, and leopards in a way that had never been done before.

2

UNBEARABLE

I had just come in from the ranch, trailed by a young lion who was attempting to eat my shoes, when the telephone rang.

"Hello. Yeah, this is he. Right, the animal man. Uh-huh. Yes, ma'am he's safe—tame as a dog. Right, next Wednesday. I'll be there. 'Bye, Miss Burke."

As I hung up, Laura, one of our stunt girls, came in.

"That call was from Billie Burke. Remember? She played Glinda, the Good Witch of the North, in *The Wizard of Oz*. She was married to Ziegfeld, of Ziegfeld Follies fame. Well, now she's got her own TV program, and she wants me to bring a bear on her next show."

Pulling the lion off my shoes, Laura said, "You told her you had a bear?"

"Yes."

"Do you?"

"No."

"So where are you going to get a bear?"

"Brian has one."

"You mean the guy who hauls the garbage?"

"Laura, he doesn't haul garbage! He picks up the day-old vegetables from the market to feed his stock! I'll give him a ring."

The next day I was on my way to Brian's ranch. His answer to me had been affirmative. He had one bear, weighing around 300 pounds, that was leash-broken and "semi-tame." As I entered his driveway, I wondered just what *semi-tame* meant.

Brian was short and stocky, with a mild disposition. His ranch was wall-to-wall garbage: there were piles upon piles of day-old and week-old garbage, dumped out in the open field for the cattle, horses, goats, sheep, lambs, pigs, chickens, ducks, camels, and llamas to pick through.

We walked over to the cage. I approached with caution. Bears are considered to be among the most dangerous animals to train; they are extremely powerful—with a strength factor of eight to one against man—and have volatile tempers. The bear's coat was a shining black, interrupted by a dark-brown patch around his neck. He was short in body, and built like a bulldog—all head, neck, and chest. His claws and fangs were intact. Still, he *seemed* to have a gentle attitude.

"He came from up north," said Brian, while gnawing on a carrot. "Some old-timer gave him to a friend of mine who was not an animal man, and he beat the shit out of him." I noticed an indentation on the bear's nose.

"That's great news," I said facetiously. "Seriously, what am I supposed to do if he acts up?"

Brian gave me a look of mock surprise. "I thought you were the famous animal trainer who can affection-train anything!" he said, giving me a wink.

"All right, never mind. I have no choice."

"When do you need him?" Brian asked.

"Tomorrow morning—and by the way, can I borrow your truck, too?"

"What's wrong with yours?" he asked.

"Blew a valve. Can't get it fixed until I get the money from the bear job."

"Sorry, ol' buddy, but I've got a market run tomorrow—can't let 'em down! They can't keep old food around, and I don't want to lose my pickup contract."

Upon returning home I made some calls for a vehicle, but to no avail. Finally, I tried Walter, a plump doughboy whose glasses kept sliding down his nose. Old Walt was a good friend, but someone I'd only call as a last resort. He hated animals!

"Hello, Wally, ol' buddy! Whadda ya mean, what do I want? Yeah, but that was *last* time! I know what the last animal did, but tree sloths aren't very intelligent, and I did *pay* for the damage to the ashtray.

"Look, Walt, I *need* your car. Mine broke down. What for? Well, you see, I've got to bring a small animal to a famous actress's TV show. What kind of animal? Well, it's a bear. Walt? . . . Walter? Hello?

"Look, Wally, it's tame, and . . . I know your car's new, but this animal is tame. I already asked everyone else. Yes, I'll put a blanket in the backseat, and yes, you can drive. Yes, I know you hate animals—don't worry, I'll keep him away from you."

We went out to Brian's early the next morning. Although I had worked with bears before, the owners had always been present. This time, I didn't even know the bear's name. Brian had left on his food run early that morning and hadn't left instructions of any kind. As I was leaving, a keeper handed me a bag of the bear's favorite cookies.

"Okay, Smoky," I said, nicknaming him. I gently put a chain around his neck. "Let's go for a ride."

I tucked a blanket on the backseat of Walt's car, and Smoky and I settled in. The bear's 300-pound body filled the back seat, squishing me into the corner. The seat under him was so mashed down that I was afraid the front of the car would lift right up from the road.

"Please watch the upholstery," Walt whined.

Off we went to the set of "The Billie Burke Show." It was an exceptionally hot August day in the San Fernando Valley, and the temperature was close to 100 degrees. I rolled the window down, letting in as much air as I could. Smoky had curled up on the seat, munching on the cookies I gave him to keep him occupied.

As we sped down the freeway, I noticed that Walt kept looking at Smoky in the rearview mirror.

"How's he doing?" he muttered nervously.

"So far, so good."

But as we headed into the Cahuenga Pass, Smoky began to repeatedly jump down from the seat to the floor and back up. His movements became more rapid, and the car began to bounce.

"What's he doing, Ralph?" Walt asked anxiously. "Something wrong? He acts nervous!"

"Oh, it's nothing," I lied. "He's just exercising." The bear had now begun to moan, something bears do when agitated. It starts in their lower throat and can build to a full-size roar. If it reaches the roar stage, you'd better have your track shoes on.

The hot summer wind was blowing into the car. Smoky was boiling, and it occurred to me that he might also be feeling carsick! His actions were now becoming frantic. Instead of jumping on the car seat, he was jumping on me, stepping on my face and head. I could see his four-inch fangs and feel his hot breath. Every time he jumped down, his daggerlike claws dug into my Levis. His moans were becoming louder.

"Ralph?!!!"

"Yes, Walt."

"We're going to die."

"Don't be stupid," I said, as a king-size paw slapped me in the face. "He's just active."

By now, Smoky clearly wanted out. He started to climb out the open window. We were doing sixty-five, and Walt, who was looking in the rearview mirror more often than he was looking at the road, was weaving all over the place. Smoky was halfway out the car window, and cars passing by were honking, their drivers yelling various things—including profanities—at us.

"The poor animal!" screamed one woman. "You quit hurting him!"

One person threw an empty beer can at us, which hit the side of the car.

"My car!" yelled Walt. "My beautiful car!"

"Don't worry about your car—just try to pull over!!"

"I can't! The freeway divides here in the middle lane, and I've got a car on each side looking at the bear!"

I was now down on my back, my feet braced against the door, pulling on Smoky with all my might. The situation was getting critical; the bear was roaring his head off.

"We're going to die, Ralph!"

"Will you shut up?!" I yelled.

The car veered abruptly, which caused Smoky to lose his balance. As he fought to right himself, he grabbed for the back of the driver's seat. With his other paw he grabbed Walt.

"Aaaaah!! Ralph! Oh, shit! *He's got me!* Ralph!! HELP!!"

The car was now practically out of control. Walt could hardly see through the bear's paws. I saw my opportunity and, grabbing the handle, rolled the window up. Then I slowly peeled Smoky's paw from Walt's red face. Walt's eyes were bulging—he was scared to death.

"Walt, get a hold of yourself!"

"I hate you," he said. "I *really* hate you!"

With the window closed, the heat was unbearable. Smoky was beside himself; the heat and carsickness were too much for him. He reached up into the corner of the car's upholstered roof, and with one swat he ripped the upholstery clean through to the metal. I shot a quick look at the rearview mirror. Walt's eyes were bugging to their limit. I saw my profit in Smoky diminishing.

The people in the cars on both sides were honking and shouting. Walt was waving at them to get out of his way so he could pull over. They just waved back. My attitude changed. I was hot, tired, and angry—a bad combination for a generally clearthinking animal behaviorist. I gathered the chain leash in my hands and jerked it down with all my might, at the same time yelling "NO!" But Smoky was beyond reason. He turned, standing fully upright in the backseat. His small, beady red eyes filled with anger. With head bent sideways against the roof, he roared defiantly, and then attacked me—all out.

Three hundred pounds of black fury sank its fangs three inches into my lower thigh. The pain was excruciating. Pulling his fangs out, the bear scraped and ripped at my leg from knee to ankle, then lay across my lap, moaning. Saliva and blood dripped from his mouth.

"Oh my God, Ralph! RALPH!!! Talk to me! Are you still there?!"

"Shut up, Walter, and just pull over!"

Walter swung the car to the right, nearly crashing into a car in the next lane. The driver screamed some obscenities. The bear just lay there on my lap as though saying, "Just one move, you bastard, and you're mine!"

"There's a gas station about a mile up the road," I said. "Let's go for it!"

Walt zoomed into the station and came to a screeching stop.

"Go get a Coke."

"A what?!" Walt screamed. "Are you crazy? I'm getting an ambulance and a doctor!"

"Wally, for Chrissake, just do as I say!" Walt jumped out, and was back in a flash with a Coke.

"Show it to the bear."

"Bullshit! You think I'm crazy!"

"Just show it to him."

I slowly opened the car door. Walt approached with the Coke. "Here, little bearie. Here you are. This is Wally, your friend!"

The bear looked up, still mad as hell. Slowly he got up off me and started toward Walt.

"Ralph! Ralph! He's coming!"

"When he gets out, just hand him the Coke."

"My God, how I hate you, Ralph! I just want to be an accountant, raise a nice family. . . ."

"Walter!!"

"Okay, okay! Come on, bearie."

The bear stepped out. Spotting the Coke, he grabbed it from Walt's hand; then he sat up, tilted the bottle back, and sucked away. I sneaked out of the car, sore and bloody. I told Walt to get five or six more Cokes. As the bear drank, he began to settle down. I walked him over to a steel-pipe fence cemented into the ground. Tying him off, I got the hose and began watering him down. It was clear that the coolness felt great to him, and he was now back to normal.

By now, a small army of people had gathered. Walt watched Smoky while I went into the bathroom to check my injuries. Easing off my stiff, blood-soaked pants, I scrubbed away until I located two fair-sized holes I could nearly stick my fingers into. I washed the wounds the best I could. The cold water stopped the bleeding. The gas station attendant gave me some bandages, which I wrapped around my thigh. My lower leg was a mass of scratches and bruises but was otherwise okay. Slipping on the clean pair of slacks that I had brought along so that I'd look presentable on stage, I walked back out.

"Walt, what time is it?"

"3:45."

"We have fifteen minutes to get to the studio."

"What?! Ralph, you're *crazy,* man! There's no way."

"Walt, listen, the bear is cool. We'll take a bunch of goodies from the vending machine to keep him busy. We're just five minutes away from the studio! My reputation is at stake!"

"Ralph, look at my car. It's *totaled!*"

"Just the interior."

"Oh! *Well!!* Just the interior?! Thanks a *lot!*"

"I didn't mean it like that. But I do need the job so I can pay you to fix it up!"

"What about *your* car?"

"Yeah, well, you're first, ol' buddy. I'm really sorry about all this."

"Okay, okay! Let's try it."

We piled the car full of junk food. Then we loaded Smoky in and took off like greased lightning. Walt was zooming through traffic like a race-car driver. I was feeding Smoky, and he was washing the food down with soft drinks as fast as he could. I took an occasional swig myself. The effects of the heat had just begun to show on Smoky again as we pulled into the studio lot.

We raced to the sound stage and walked in just as the show was starting. Miss Burke walked out onto the stage in a beautiful evening dress with a high, frilled lace collar. Her blonde curls framed the warmth of her smile. The assistant told me that when my name was called, I was to just walk out with the bear. Billie would ask me some questions, I was to make the bear sit up or something, and that would be it.

Finally, the director signaled me to walk on. I entered with Smoky, who seemed to be quite calm. Billie's dialogue for this segment was not short-lived, however. On the contrary, it went on and on—she chatted about show business, about the role animals play in it, and about the life story of Smoky the Bear.

By now, Smoky wanted to go home—*right away*. He started to moan and then began to pull on his chain. I saw Walt, standing offstage, wince. Billie, unaware of what was going on, continued her chatter. While I was talking, smiling, and, I hoped, laughing at the appropriate times, I jerked back on Smoky's chain. That was my last mistake. Quick as a flash, he bit me on the hand. Fortunately, the camera was on Billie, and the TV audience didn't see it. I started to bleed, so I quickly thrust my hand into my pocket and bled into my handkerchief. With the other hand, I attempted to control Smoky, who by now was thrashing about and becoming very obnoxious. Billie, in her refined way, laughed and said, "Oh! The dear boy is so cute! Koochie-koochie!"

Smoky was reaching his boiling point and I was preparing for the worst. I saw him stand up, with the same look on his face that I'd seen before. His ears were back, and his red, beady eyes were aflame. Suddenly, from out of nowhere, a huge pizza came whizzing across the stage and landed at Smoky's feet. Dropping down on all fours, he began to eat. It was a real lifesaver.

When the show ended, I reached Walt and asked where the pizza had come from.

"From me," beamed Walt. "Well, from the prop man, that is. They had a pizza commercial coming up. I grabbed one of the pizzas and threw the prop man a few bucks."

"It was just in time, Walt. I owe you one!"

"You just owe me one new interior."

"As soon as I get the money. Buddy, you're the best."

"On second thought, Ralph, keep the money and fix *your* car. Then I won't ever have to worry about your asking to borrow mine again!"

As for Smoky, I returned him to Brian early that evening. Brian didn't seem all that happy to get him back, but I sure wasn't sorry to see him go. As I drove to the hospital to get my leg stitched up, I hoped that the next call I got would be for a trained raccoon.

3

STOMPED

We received a call one day to do a commercial for the *Yellow Pages* phone directory. The commercial called for an ostrich to stand in a telephone booth in the middle of the desert and, on command, run out.

I had a beautiful pair of ostriches. However, the hen had just laid a clutch of eggs, and she and the male were taking turns sitting on the nest. I sure didn't want to upset them. My wife Toni had just successfully developed a hatching-and-caring program that gave us about 70 percent live births—a bit unusual, since the survival rate for ostriches is generally less than half that.

Fortunately, a good friend of mine, Gene Holter, had a fairly large group of ostriches that ran wild on his ranch with other exotic animals. After a quick call to him, I was on my way to pick two out; one as the lead bird and the other as his double.

Gene specialized in supplying animal acts to circuses and carnivals. A large piece of land behind his house was home to about a hundred head of exotic stock—eland, zebras, camels, Barbary sheep, and, of course, a group of ostriches, of which eight were females and three male. None of the animals were tame—that is to say, while they were calm and collected when in the enclosure, no one could get very close. To be touched would be very stressful for them.

Gene was on the phone when I arrived, but he motioned me toward the back of the house. "I'll join you as soon as I'm off," he told me. I nodded an okay and headed back.

A six-foot-tall chain-link fence encircled the area. The fence had a foot or two of barbed wire running around the top as a deterrent to anyone who might want to take a closer look at the animals.

I unlatched the gate and walked in. Most of the animals looked up from their grazing for a moment, then continued their munching, content that I wasn't going to harm them.

Halfway across, I noticed the ostriches, all grouped together, hunting and pecking as they moved. As I edged over to them, I saw that the largest male had stopped eating and was standing tall, eyeing my movements. A big male ostrich can weigh 300 pounds and stand some eight feet tall (the females are about a quarter less in size).

As I approached, the rest of the group moved away, keeping about thirty feet between us. The male stood his ground, just watching. I knew that males could get pretty tough during the breeding season, but I saw no signs of this behavior; also, I knew the season was a couple of months away.

I skirted the perimeter of the birds, checking out which ones looked the best—heavy weighted, good color, alert. I saw what I was looking for in two birds who were off together. Their markings were identical. They even seemed to walk alike, preening at the same time. "True twins," I laughed to myself, and turned around to head back. Standing directly behind me, about ten feet away, was the big cock bird.

Now I could really see how massive he was. I stood there for a moment, not quite understanding this unusual behavior. Then I started to move toward the gate. He followed immediately, in a parallel line. I stopped, turned slowly, and walked in the opposite direction to see if his "following" me had been a coincidence. But sure enough, he turned and followed me again.

I had only a few choices: to walk directly away toward the fence line, to *run* toward the fence, or to bluff him.

Usually, an ostrich can be "shooed" away with the wave of a hand, but this bird was acting very weirdly. I knew that one should only rarely run away from any exotic animal that is showing an interest. It usually entices the animal to chase you, and, let's face it, these animals can outrun you any time. In this case, I knew that an ostrich can run with the speed of a racehorse—at some forty-five miles an hour—so I decided to *walk* away.

As I headed for the fence, I could hear those bone-crunching feet behind me, getting closer with each step. This bird was moments away from attacking me! Why, I didn't know—but I *did* know that he had the capability of killing me. An ostrich's legs—two huge, three-toed, pounding clubs—are its weapons. One well-placed blow can disembowel a man. The bill isn't a problem; even a hard peck and a twisting bite will draw only a little blood, but will do no more serious damage.

I figured the only chance I had was to bluff. If I just had a stick that was long enough to press against his chest, or a forked one for his neck, I would be out of danger. But the field was sandy and rocky, with no such sticks in sight.

I stopped, took a deep breath, turned, and ran straight at him, yelling and waving my arms. He straightened his neck, shooting his head straight up, towering over me. His wings shot out; he filled his plumage. With his mouth open, he hissed like a snake, and, first standing on his tiptoes, he charged.

I couldn't believe he would have the audacity. I turned and was gone, racing away as fast as I could. Having Western boots on at a time like this didn't help matters! I plunged directly into the group of ostriches, scattering them in all directions. "Old Fred," as I was to find out later was his name, was right behind me, raking at me with those giant feet. I knew that if I tripped and went down, I would be in serious trouble. Those two great, powerful legs gave him a great advantage in the world of animals. He could pivot on a dime, and he'd never lose his momentum, thanks to the balance of his outstretched wings.

A quick look at the fence told me I was too far away to reach it before he would have me. I started to jig and jog left and right, but he was really after my hide. Running into his girlfriends had not helped. Dust was flying in all directions. One of his feet caught me on the downstroke, ripping my leather jacket literally in two and sending me flying. I did a "tuck and roll," thanking God for my stunt training, and landed on my feet. Then I was off again, cutting this way and that.

The big toe in the center of the ostrich's foot is the one that

31

does the damage. The claw was huge, hard, and sharp. Whenever I stopped and started to dodge the bird, I could see his foot stomping on the ground near me. The huge footprints in the sand looked like those of a giant pterodactyl. My tactics were edging me closer to the fence, but not close enough for me to make a break for it.

Then I tripped! My foot went into a gopher hole, and down I went. The bird was right on top of me. His feet came down in fast repetition. He caught my jacket with one foot, pinning me to the ground, and started to rip it to shreds with his other foot.

Rolling over, I managed to get one arm out of the sleeve, but not before the big toe slashed across my shoulder like a razor, opening up an eight-inch gash. I rolled over and, freeing my other arm, stood up.

Like a bull goring a matador, the ostrich was ripping and tearing the jacket to pieces, thinking in his primitive brain that I was still inside it, or at least that it was part of me. I headed for the fence. After only a few yards, though, the ostrich came after me again, striking out and hissing, wings spread. I decided to go for it. My strength was running out. It was now or never.

Clothes ripped, with blood oozing down my arm and leg, I took off. That fence seemed a mile away. I could hear only my own breathing and the hissing and stomping of the bird. A kick caught me in the back, then caught my belt, and down I went. This time the bird got me good, right across the fleshy part of my upper leg. I was now blood spattered, and my clothes were torn. I got up again, knowing I *had* to make it, or else. A headline flashed through my mind: "Hollywood Stuntman Killed by Bird!" That did it. I neared the fence, hit it four feet off the ground, and scrambled up and over, falling flat on my back—safely on the other side.

The bird hit the fence full and bounced back, falling down. He scrambled to his feet and charged me through the fence again and again, to no avail. I heard Gene yelling from afar and knew that he was on the way—unfortunately, a bit late.

I hobbled to my feet. For the first time I realized I had gone over the barbed wire at the top of the fence. Blood poured from about ten small holes and gouges in my hands and arms. I was rigging a tourniquet when Gene arrived.

"Good Lord, Ralph!! What in the world . . . !" Gene helped me up and threw one of my arms over his shoulder as we headed back. "The best I can figure out is an off-season heat," he said. "Sometimes in captivity, animals go through their natural breeding cycle at odd times. That would certainly account for this guy's behavior.

"Come on in and clean up, and I'll run you over to the hospital. If you're hungry, we can grab a bite out of the fridge and take it with us."

"What have you got?"

"Turkey."

"No, thanks!"

✳

A week later, my trainers and I were on our way to Death Valley. We had chosen a large bird who did *not* have the "killer instinct." He was eight feet tall, weighed 250 pounds, and had gorgeous black and white plumage.

We had the crew work quietly; these large birds are very flighty, and the smallest noises can set them off. Before taking the ostrich out of the trailer, we put a black hood over his head to prevent him from seeing something that might startle him. Only his beak poked through.

It took four of us to "convince" him to "walk" over to the booth. This was accomplished by locking our arms under his body and practically picking him up! Once he was placed in the booth, we slid a pan of grain into a fake open telephone book. Then, upon getting an okay from the director, we took off the hood and carefully crept out of the shot. The old boy began to peck at the grain. It looked for all the world as though he were searching for a telephone number in the book!

The director whispered to me to have the bird move out of the booth. We threw a full bucket of grain down about ten feet outside the booth. The bird saw it, but he stayed in the booth, still pecking at the telephone book. About thirty seconds went by, and the director began to get desperate. One of the crew, thinking he would help, walked over to a nearby pickup truck, quietly opened the door, and then slammed it shut!

The bird's head shot straight up. In one stride he was out the door, and a minute later he was gone from view. He must have been doing forty miles an hour as he raced up one side of a sand dune and down the other. The last we saw of him before he disappeared from view was a tiny head bobbing against the blue sky.

It took a helicopter and two days of intense searching to find him. He was holed up in the backyard of a small farm. When we drove up, he was in the chicken yard, hunting and pecking with his smaller kin as though he had been born and raised there.

At least the director had gotten his shot!

4

ZAMBA

I woke up slowly, aware of a heavy weight pressing me down into the bed. It felt as though a car had slipped off its jack and pinned me to the ground. I opened my eyes—well, one eye (the other was smashed shut)—and all I could see was this huge mass of hair lying on me. Zamba never could sleep on *his* side of the bed. Sure, he would start there, but by morning he had found himself a more comfortable place, lying across my wife Toni and me. Although he had his own sleeping arrangement in his cage outside with the other animals, we occasionally allowed him to join us as a special treat. We had built a special bed, far larger than king-size, to accommodate two average-sized people and one 528-pound African lion. Heavy-duty construction and springs kept Zamba from falling through.

The lion's huge paw over my face convinced me that today would be bath day for him. Arching my back, I managed to slip myself out from under his massive frame. Toni had already gotten up, and I could smell the coffee. In the years since our marriage, she had been a true supporter and partner. She was Diana the huntress and Venus the love goddess rolled into one— tall, with long blonde hair, green eyes, and a regal bearing. After a quick shower, I dressed, ignoring shaving. This was Sunday. Zamba, lying diagonally across the bed, was still asleep, snoring his head off.

I kicked the bed. "Zam! Come on! Up and out!"

He rose up, with his huge mane matted to the back of his head. One eye was half-closed. He looked as though he'd had a night on the town. He gave me an "Oh, it's you" look and flopped back on the bed. I headed for the kitchen.

Toni surprised me with a special Sunday breakfast—ham, bacon, eggs over easy, toast, jam, hash browns, and a romantic kiss. "Isn't this great!" I thought. True, we didn't have a lot of money—in fact, very little. But we had the animals, a unique way of life, and each other.

We heard a thud as something hit the ground, and knew it was Zamba getting out of bed. He dragged himself sleepily into the kitchen, ignoring the yapping of our new Rhodesian Ridgeback puppy. He tripped over Speedy the tortoise, banged the back-door screen open with his head, and headed for his favorite tree—which was starting to show the use.

Over coffee we chatted about the day's activities, which centered around finishing up all the loose ends left over from the week.

Raunchy, the jaguar, had crunched the corner of his nine-gauge chain-link cage into metal shavings, and I knew that if another day went by he'd be out. Titan, our resident falcon, needed to have his claws clipped. And above all, Zamba needed a bath. To bathe a lion—ha! It's better to try to bathe a bevy of kids.

The morning was a bit crisp, so I decided to give Zamba his bath at noon, when the sun's heat was at its fullest. I'd take care of Titan and Raunchy first.

The falcons' flight cage was quite large, having been built over a small forest to allow the birds a natural setting. This made it possible for them to fly a considerable distance, unhampered. Slipping on my gauntlet, I entered the cage. Holding a piece of meat between my fingers, I whistled for Titan. He launched off a tree from about 30 feet in the air, and in one smooth, graceful swoop he landed on my gloved hand. I immediately offered him the tidbit of meat, which he accepted and ate ravenously.

He was a falcon of incredible beauty. His black and silver feathers shone in the morning sun; his alert, piercing eyes saw every movement instantly.

Carefully, I ran my hand over his back and enclosed his wings.

Turning him over, I cradled him in my arm, holding the talon in my hand. I called to Toni to come in and bring the clippers. Carefully, so as not to be grabbed accidentally by the remaining talon, in one expert move, she gently snipped away the overgrown nail.

I righted Titan on my gloved hand. He stretched his wings for balance and preened them in place. Then, as though he had completed *his* mission, he soared off into the trees.

With this done, we went to work rethreading the chain-link in Raunchy's cage. We worked hard for a couple of hours, but as it was approaching noon and we had only a little bit left to do, we figured we'd give Zamba his bath and finish the cage afterward.

I tied Zamba to a nearby tree before bringing out the garden hose. I knew that once he saw it, he'd be gone if he could. His eyes grew as big as saucers. He moved to the end of his chain and tested it with his weight, but there was no escape!

I filled a bucket with baby shampoo and threw in a bar of soap for good measure. Knowing that when Zamba got a bath, I got a bath, I took off everything but my shorts. Then I approached the "king of beasts."

All hell broke loose! Zamba roared, ran, and jumped, but to no avail. Each time he passed by me, I had to leap over the chain. "Come on, you big baby! If you want to sleep in our bed, you've got to take a bath!"

Zamba perked up his ears at my voice and, as if he understood and was resigned to his fate, flopped down and rested his chin on the ground. Then we (Toni, wisely attired in a bathing suit, had come out to help) went to work. First, the hose. Using a strong spray, always pointed away from his face, we hosed Zamba down completely. Next, we poured a bucket of soap and water into his thick mane and over his entire body. That was followed by three or four more bucketfuls. Then Toni and I went to work with the brushes, scrubbing away on every inch of his body.

Zamba seemed to take to that part, but when it came time for us to wash his face, he squinted his eyes and pouted. We poured water gently over his scrunched-up, sourpuss face and, using a sponge, carefully wiped it off. After we had cleaned each eye, he would open it, revealing a searching orb, which would then close tight in anticipation of the next stroke.

The mane was another matter. Ten inches thick and matted, the multicolored, coarse hair hung in wet sheets, heavy with water and suds. Zamba looked like the proverbial drowned rat. For well over an hour we picked, preened, brushed, and combed. Zamba's will was now broken. He just accepted it—although I do truly believe he loved the fuss (with the exception of the face cleaning!).

Toni went into the house and brought out a dozen towels. I moved Zamba over to a dry spot, and we rubbed him down thoroughly. The first six towels were soaked quickly, but by the second half they were starting to come away dry. Zamba stood up and shook himself, spraying us with the last few drops.

Then out came the comb. This was a specially made, foot-long comb with two-inch teeth, all the better to get into that thick mane. As we combed, the mane became full and soft. The hot August sun was starting to warm Zamba's tawny skin, and steam was rising from his back. His eyes, no longer threatened with soap and water, were opened wide. The reflection of all creation seemed to be there. He was so beautiful.

Toni and I had fastened a steel cable about eight feet off the ground between two oak trees. The ground there had been raked and cleaned, and heavy cedar chips had been laid down. I fastened Zamba's chain to a clip, then attached the clip to a ring that slid the length of the cable. This allowed Zamba to exercise the full length of the cable. If he decided to rest, the cedar chips would absorb any dampness, as well as keep him clean.

Once on the cable, he shook himself again. Then, feeling cocky as a puppy, he proceeded to race up and down the run, grunting and cavorting and just plain feeling good. He was breathtaking. I felt so proud of him. He was the perfect example of affection training—the living proof that man and animal—specifically, a carnivorous animal—can live together, coexisting in man's environment; that the animal could, *by choice,* change his way of life, not for one that he liked better, but for one that he enjoyed equally. When he wanted something, he let his wants be known, and his needs were met. His beautiful fangs and sharp claws grew long from lack of use in this new society. Zamba was a full-grown adult male, in prime condition. His skin glowed in the natural earth colors—creams, light and dark browns, black, ocher, and burnt orange. Now he sat on a small rise, head alert, as though he were looking far into his past. His ears were pricked forward, and with his tail he twitched at an occasional fly.

I called his name. He lowered his ears for just a moment, and I heard a small throaty noise in response, but then his ears shot back up. A slight breeze blew wisps of his mane. We left him to warm himself and relax in the afternoon sun.

✳

Heading back to the compound, we went to work on the jaguar's cage. It took only a few minutes to complete. I put the last clamp on the chain-link fence as Toni headed for the kitchen to prepare lunch. I checked the cage for a moment, feeling pretty good about our handiwork. Raunchy got up and padded back and forth, ready to go home. I unclipped his chain, opened the cage door, and let him inside. He immediately headed over to the spot we had been working on. Smelling and sniffing, he checked it out thoroughly. I slipped the chain off, patted his massive head, stepped out and locked the door. Then I headed for the house. By the aroma, I could tell that Toni had the hamburgers and onions well on the way.

Before lunch I washed off as much of the sweat and dirt as I could. Turning off the faucet, I braced my hands on the sink and looked into the mirror. Suddenly, a searing ache of terror consumed me. *Something was wrong!*

Zamba!! I raced toward the kitchen.

Toni was standing there in the middle of the floor, the spatula still hanging in her hand, her mouth open, eyes staring. She had always sensed my pain.

"Zamba!" I screamed. We ran toward the front door, crashing it open. "Oh, my God!"

The worst sight imaginable greeted our eyes.

"Dear God! Zamba!"

He was hanging by his neck over the steel cable, bent and lifeless, his head on one side, his body draped on the other, his hind section and tail dragging on the ground. Somehow, he had run around the oak tree, leaped eight feet up and over the wire, and been unable to get back.

As we ran to him, my mind was racing. How long had he been there? A minute? Five? Maybe even ten! His gorgeous, lifeless eyes stared at me. I touched them. They were sticky and unblinking.

I grabbed the clip to release the pressure from around Zamba's neck, but the tension was too strong. Toni and I tried to lift him over the wire to release the pressure of the chain around his neck, but his weight was too much for us.

"Zamba, baby!" Toni cried.

I was frantic. We had to *do* something, now! But what?

I ran around the other side and, reaching over, grabbed his mane, one leg, and the bulk of his body and pulled for all I was worth—an impossible task.

"Come on, big fella!" I gasped.

Toni got underneath, and we gave it all we had. The enormous body moved, slid, swayed. I felt numbing pain as something tore in my arm. I pulled. Toni pushed. The balance shifted. Zamba's lifeless body teetered and then fell on me, knocking me flat.

I scrambled out from underneath him and, digging my hand into his mane, found the chain that was tight around his throat, choking off his windpipe. I squeezed the clip to release the pressure, and the whole chain popped off.

We pried Zamba's mouth open. His tongue and gums were white. Then I tapped his eye . . . no response.

"He's dead, Toni. Zamba's dead."

The emotion was too much. I burst into tears. "My Zamba! My baby—he *couldn't!* He can't. Please, dear God!!"

He had been my mentor, my guide into the world of nature, my companion.

"We shouldn't have left him!" Toni sobbed. But for years we, like everybody else, had always tied our animals out. There had never been a problem. This was some kind of freak accident.

Toni wrapped her arms around the lion and hugged him as if her heart would break. Her weight pressed air from his lungs. When I heard it, I flung my full weight on his body, and again another small volume of air burst forth.

"Toni, honey, press together with me."

He was so huge that it took the full pressure of both our bodies to force the release of air from his lungs.

"Oh, Ralph, can it really help??"

"I don't know—but we have to try *something!*"

We were exhausted, but we wouldn't give up. For twenty minutes we pushed and released. I kept Zamba's mouth open, his tongue out, to free the passageway, but Toni's and my pushing ended only with our being completely drained. We lay there, Toni with her head in Zamba's mane, whimpering softly. I had my head buried in his chest, too depressed to move.

"It's no use," I said.

Our breathing slowed. I was afraid to rise, to look into those eyes.

Then I heard it!

I pressed my ear tightly to his chest and listened.

"What's wrong, Ralph?"

"Sshh!" I whispered.

Then I heard it again! A far-off, slow, nearly inaudible beat. A *heartbeat!*

"Oh, my God, it's *beating!*" I heard it down there, in that mess of hair. Inside that great body, I heard it.

I started to rub Zamba all over to help his circulation. Toni joined in. We didn't even feel our previous exhaustion. Grabbing all four of his feet, we rolled him over onto his other side and continued rubbing. A quick look in his mouth told me that his color was coming back.

I had Toni bring blankets from the house. I wrapped them all around his body for heat while she went to call the vet.

"He's on the way!" she yelled, running to crash down beside me. We hugged and kissed Zamba and each other.

I slowly reached up toward Zamba's eye and, taking a deep breath, touched it. It blinked! Dear God! He was alive! Both Toni and I began to cry, shedding tears of joy and of deep, heartfelt gratitude.

When the vet arrived, he immediately administered intravenous injections and stimulants and started glucose and drip salines. Artificial heat was applied to keep Zamba's temperature up.

"What happened, Ralph?" the vet asked as he worked.

I told him what I thought had happened.

"How long were you away?"

"Just a matter of minutes!"

"Has this ever happened to you before?"

"Never, and I've never heard of it happening to anyone else. That's what these cable runs are for—to allow the animals freedom to run and play."

"Well, it's a miracle he's still alive. He must have done it moments before you walked out."

After a couple of hours, the vet left, giving us instructions that would keep us busy for the rest of the night. We set up camp outside around Zamba, since the doctor thought it best not to move him. Sundown brought hot Santa Ana breezes, drifting in from the high desert. The stars were brilliant, the night balmy.

Neighbors and friends had come from miles around to help in any way they could. These were people who had known Zamba since he was a baby. They came with blankets, fruit, all kinds of food. They had automatically planned on staying for the night, or even for a week, if necessary. All of the people there were dedicated lovers of nature—its forests, oceans, mountains, jungles, and especially its living creatures. We cried for its pain and loss.

We all took turns keeping the fire going, and the men assisted me in turning Zamba every half-hour to prevent the buildup of fluid in his peritoneal cavity. I checked constantly to see that the intravenous needle hadn't slipped out of the vein.

As the evening wore on, a circle of people formed around the fire. Some of the kids got sleepy and gently cuddled up to Zamba for warmth. We watched closely so they wouldn't disturb him.

Zamba loved kids. My young daughter Tana had been brought up with him and many times had fallen asleep deeply embedded in his mane. Tana, who was named after a river in Kenya, was the image of her mother. She was probably one of the few children who have ever had a lion around as one would have a dog; it was not uncommon to see her riding on his back across the nearby valleys. She would often brush him to sleep, combing his mane.

I was lying against a tree with Zamba's head on my lap, when he suddenly moaned. What rapture to my ears! I petted him and stroked his head and kept talking to him, reassuring him of all the good things to come.

Zamba slept peacefully most of the night, but I kept waking him up to see if he was okay. Morning found him staggering, trying to get up. A couple of the men and I supported his weight, and we were finally able to get his legs underneath him. Then, like a drunken sailor in a stupor, he started to walk. He was headed for the oak tree, and we turned him just in time to keep him from hitting his head.

For the rest of that day, he stood up periodically and walked in a tight circle for a bit, then collapsed and slept for a while. By the day's end, we had him in the kitchen, one of his favorite spots. He loved to lie on the cold stone floor and smell the cooking. It looked as though he was out of danger and well on the way to recovery.

✸

It was early in the morning of the third day. I had gotten up to see how Zamba was doing. He lay sprawled against the wall, and I crept along quietly so as not to wake him. But in making the coffee, I accidentally knocked over a cup. The sound caused Zamba to wake up quickly.

"Morning, Zam. Had a nice rest?" I asked.

He responded by yawning and stretching, and then proceeded to come to me. But he walked right into the cabinet, banging his head on the door.

Strange, I thought. I stepped around behind him and called again. "Come on, boy, over here." He turned a quarter-turn and headed toward me at a forty-five-degree angle. Missing me by six feet, he walked right into the wall.

"Oh, no! *Toni!*" I yelled. "Toni!"

She appeared in the hall. "What's wrong?" she asked.

"I think Zamba's blind!!"

The vet confirmed my fears. Zamba was totally blind. The vet explained that when the chain had closed off Zamba's air passage, the optic nerves had also been squeezed. He said that this was not uncommon in this type of accident.

"Will he ever see again?" I asked, brushing my hand over Zamba's eyes.

"He could—one never knows. It depends on the severity of the injury."

"Well, it was pretty severe, wouldn't you say?" I asked him.

"Yes, but that massive mane helped cushion it. Time will tell."

Toni and I massaged Zamba's throat every few hours, day after day, and administered his medicine religiously. Although he seemed to be getting stronger, we noticed no improvement in his vision. Most mornings we would lead him out into the field alongside the house, where he would "look" off into the distance. How wonderful is the ability of animals to accept their problems! No moaning, no self-pity—just acceptance and quiet dignity.

We learned quickly that a "Harrumph!" from Zamba meant that he had to "visit" his tree. I would put a canvas harness around his chest, similar to that used for seeing-eye dogs. Then, with Zamba pressing hard against my leg, he and I would walk outside. After a while, I didn't even need to use a harness. If he was touching my leg, that was sufficient for him to feel secure.

We would take long walks up the slope. For the most part, Zamba's gait was smooth and graceful; occasionally he would stumble, but only for a moment. At the top, Zamba would first sit on his haunches and gaze off into the distance, and then he'd lie down in the soft green of the field.

I would comb his mane with my fingers. Countless times I said I was sorry, but each time hurt as much as the first. It seemed that he always forgave, never questioning, never hesitating in his love for me. To have his kind of peace of mind, to accept all without question . . . how I struggled at those moments to penetrate his mind to find the knowledge he possessed so naturally. He had the ability to turn all things into a positive. He was born with that acceptance, as were his father and his forefathers, on and on, back to the origins of animalkind. We are of one world, he and I, and yet he feels a different wind blowing. The smell of the great outdoors is scented for his nostrils only. He sees with his third eye, and the roar of his voice answers questions unknown to us to ask.

Why is this so? Animals have attained such perfection in their existence, while man has never known such tranquility. I have always believed that animals listen to one perfect voice—nature's voice—and do as it bids them. We, on the other hand, listen only to ourselves, and we do as we please. Our ego, our pride, is generally our instructor, instead of reality, intellect, or even common sense. We live our lives superficially, led by our personalities.

Zamba lay with his toes touching mine, as he now always did in bed. It was his way of knowing whether I was leaving, as he didn't want to be left alone. Now I lay with my head flat on the grass, across from him, looking into those huge eyes. I wanted so badly for him to see again, for the energy and forces of his nature to restore his sight, that by our connecting powers we could, together, put those entities to work. I've always believed that the mind rules the physical body, and that if we could only penetrate to the subconscious, we could tell our minds to instruct our bodies to *heal*. We headed down the hill.

✳

One evening I had gone to bring Zamba in from his small hilltop in the field. I thought for a moment about how he used to play: I would get down really low and make a clicking noise with my tongue. This was his signal to "act" like a lion. His ears would flatten out, and his chin would be on the ground. He would wait,

45

with his tail twitching and his body all tense. Then I would break into a run, and he would explode in an all-out race. Leaping high, he would pounce on me, knocking me flat, and . . . lick my face. It had been good fun. I took a deep breath. "At least he's still alive," I murmured to myself.

As I walked toward him, I noticed that his head was down, his tail was twitching, and his ears were flat. He was stalking me! But how . . . his eyes . . . could it be possible?

I bent low and, praying to God, made the clicking noise with my tongue. In an instant, Zamba was racing toward me full tilt. I raced away, leaping with joy. He could see again!

He caught me in midair. We hit the ground together, rolling over and over in a soft field of grass. I pulled his great head to me and kissed both his eyes.

"I love you, Zam. God, how I love you."

5

EVERYTHING'S DUCKY

"Ralph," said the assistant director, "I'd like you to meet Buddy Hackett and Mickey Rooney. Ralph's the duck trainer on your picture, guys. Ralph, show them your buddy, Herbie."

I was carrying Herbie under my arm. He let out a few quack greetings. There were handshakes all around . . . and then I noticed a look of disgust creeping across their faces. I had forgotten that I had some duck droppings on my hand.

"Sorry, fellas—that's show business, I guess!" I said apologetically.

Buddy and Mickey hung their hands out to dry as they walked away. "Sure kid, sure—we'll meet your 'loose' friend some other time!" I heard them murmur something like "weird, real weird" as they disappeared around the corner, still carrying their hands as if they were signaling for left turns.

I had been hired to supply a duck to be the lead animal in the movie *Everything's Ducky.* It was quite an honor, not only to be given the job, but also to work with these two great comedians.

In order to be prepared for anything, I had brought four ducks with me. Herbie was the principal duck actor, and the other three were his "doubles." All had been specially trained. For continuity purposes, the four were identical: they were pure white, with yellow-orange bills, and they all waddled alike and quacked alike. Almost no one could tell them apart. To the expert eye, however, they all had their own idiosyncrasies, and we named them accordingly. Burp Adenoids ("Burp," for short) hiccupped a lot, and Flops was always falling down. Duster's tail never stopped wagging. Then, of course, there was Herbie.

Although Herbie didn't trip, burp, or have a tail-wagging problem, he defecated a lot . . . a whole lot. He couldn't honk without dropping. When Herbie was around, there were duck droppings everywhere. The crew was forever slipping and sliding on it. There was one scene in which Buddy had to make a hasty entrance. He came running onto the set, hit a patch of Herbie's leavings, and proceeded to slide all the way through and out the other side.

The film was being shot on location at the Sportsman's Lodge, a restaurant in California's San Fernando Valley that specialized in serving trout that the customers had caught themselves. At the back of the restaurant was a myriad of waterfalls, bridges, and exotic greenery. Hundreds of beautiful rainbow trout swam lazily through the small ponds and streams. Guests were given poles, bait, and any paraphernalia needed to trick the trout into taking that last fatal bite. The cost of the dinner was determined by the fish's length. When a catch had been made, the happy fisherman received a number and was shown to his table to wait for his dinner to be cooked. We were there on Sundays, when the restaurant was closed.

Buddy and Mickey were always playing practical jokes on each other. In one scene, the camera followed them as they walked by the lake, talking, with Herbie tucked neatly under Buddy's arm. All of a sudden, Buddy's face screwed up like a prune, and I knew what had happened—Herbie had dropped another! Buddy, being the great actor that he is, nonchalantly continued his dialogue, while he calmly put his newly christened hand on Mickey's shoulder as they strolled. Only after the scene was over and Mickey was back in his dressing room did he realize what Buddy had done. Mickey went screaming out of his trailer, looking for Buddy . . . who was, of course, nowhere to be found.

The time came to shoot Herbie's most important scene. The script called for a drunk duck—that is to say, one who was able to *act* drunk. Buddy and Mickey were to go into a bar with Herbie, get snockered, and then leave, staggering all over the place. Ducks, although erratic in their movement, are quite steady on their feet. It had taken my head trainer, Mike, many months to train Herbie to stagger. When we heard the assistant director yell for Herbie, we knew his big moment had come.

Even though I had seen Herbie staggering around at the ranch during his training period, I was quite concerned. I knew that the lights and activity of a film production can be distracting. The director came over to brief us.

"Okay, fellas, this is how we're gonna do it. Buddy, Mickey, and Herbie will all be sitting at the bar drinking. Herbie, of course, will use a straw. When I give the cue, the three of them will get off their stools and weave, stagger, and trip all the way to the bar doors and out. Got it? Fine, let's roll it."

Then the assistant director yelled, "Quiet on the set. Roll cameras."

On the director's order for "Action," the three actors sitting at the bar began drinking, Herbie slurping away through his straw. Then Buddy and Mickey got up, staggering and weaving, and started out the door. Herbie jumped down and headed after them, walking the straightest line I've ever seen. His only irregular movement was to release his bowels twice before reaching the door.

"*Cut!*" screamed the director, following this with four or five vulgar terms relating to the duck's unscripted activity.

The scene was tried five more times, and five times Herbie walked the straight and narrow, never staggering for one moment. Mike was beside himself, as was I. Everything had gone so smoothly on the picture until now.

The assistant director yelled, "Take five!" and we exited the area, with the director ranting in the background about his picture "going to the dogs" and being "for the birds."

For some time, the trainers and I were in a huddle around a huge fake rock. Suddenly Buddy came running up.

"Hey, Ralph, you're terrific! He's doing it—the little bastard's *doing* it!"

We all looked at each other, stupefied, and then ran to the duck pen. Sure enough, there was Herbie, staggering around in figure eights, stepping on his own toes and falling forward on his bill. Even his honk sounded more like a hiccup. We raced to the director, who promptly rolled the cameras. Herbie was finally immortalized, as the *three* great comedians staggered out the barroom door.

The only problem was that even after the director had yelled "Cut," Herbie kept falling on his face. He was fast asleep and snoring up a storm within two minutes of being put in his pen.

To this day, I still don't know *exactly* what happened. But as we were leaving the set, I saw Buddy sneaking around the backdrop, carrying what appeared to be a small vodka bottle and an eyedropper.

"Buddy, you didn't!" I yelled, and I'll always remember that wonderful "apple doll" expression on Buddy's face, as though to say, "Who, *me?*"

6

AFFECTION TRAINING

As you've been reading this book, you may have been think-ing, having an exotic animal doesn't sound that difficult. Think of how much satisfaction you can get, how much love and devotion!

While it is true that raising and training exotic animals is extremely rewarding—after all, I've devoted my entire life to the beauty of the beasts—it is by no means easy. In fact, it is down-right dangerous, not only to you, but to everyone with whom you associate.

Keeping a wild animal in captivity doesn't mean that you have domesticated him. He still remains instinctively wild, although his attitude toward civilization has changed as he has learned to accept his "unnatural" surroundings. But if something occurs that threatens his existence, you could experience all that he is in the wild—right in your living room. Therefore, I strongly oppose any nonprofessional person's possessing an exotic animal. Before I share with you the essence of affection training, I'll describe some of the many difficulties in possessing an exotic animal, should this still be something you're considering.

Ownership of an exotic animal does not guarantee a positive relationship with the animal. Just as a marriage certificate has no "emotional clause" guaranteeing love, so an ownership certificate does not ensure a deep emotional bond between the animal and its owner.

In addition to having greater acuteness in the five senses, animals have a "sixth sense" that is far above our intuition.

Animals can sense your intentions toward them even before you've formulated them yourself!

Not all people can work with animals successfully. There seems to be a special "aura" needed to be able to communicate with our co-earthlings. Although I believe that everyone has a natural capacity to work with animals, only some people have a real gift for gaining an animal's trust and respect.

Not everyone wants to possess an exotic animal for the right reason. Some people want an exotic pet as a substitute for the love they didn't get as children or aren't getting in their adult lives. While love is not a bad motivation for wanting an exotic companion, love alone—without other important factors—can create a "spoiled" animal, and a spoiled animal is a dangerous animal. When an animal is young, you *give* it what you like; when it grows older, it *takes* what it likes.

An equally inappropriate reason for having an exotic animal is as a way to bolster your ego. Such people use their pets to show off, hoping that by having the animals they can attract people to them.

There are, certainly, some *valid* reasons for having an exotic animal. But even if your motivations are entirely positive, it is essential that you be professionally trained and possess that special "aura" that allows the animal to let you into its heart.

Having a big backyard or a professionally designed cage is not the only prerequisite for possessing an exotic. You must also be aware of local zoning laws, as these often prohibit the possession of wild animals in residential areas.

Local health and police authorities also have a say in how you keep your animal. State and federal laws govern the sizes and types of cages that can be used to house these pets, and special permits are needed if the animals are on the endangered list (and note that this can be an extremely expensive proposition). All in all, I believe strongly in most of these regulations. For a person who truly wants an exotic, it is best to live in a remote area.

Some of the greatest difficulties in possessing an exotic animal come as the animal grows into maturity. When exotics are young, they are quite cuddly and easy to handle, but as the months go by, they can become very dangerous. There have been numerous tragic cases of wild-animal "pets" in the house attacking and mauling their owners. In some cases, a member of the family or a friend has been killed or dismembered. A young couple who had had a cougar as a house pet for years were horrified when, out of jealousy and because it had not been professionally raised, the animal bit the fingers off their newborn baby as the child's hand dangled over the edge of the crib. In another case, when a woman who kept a lion tried to pet it through the cage, it attacked her, dismembering her arm.

Even the innocent-looking chimpanzee can wreak havoc in the home. In point of fact, professionals consider a chimp to be *potentially more dangerous than a lion.* Because chimps have engaging, humanlike qualities and natural intelligence, people tend to be less on guard around them than around other wild animals.

While many of the unfortunate owners who become the victims of such accidents are well meaning and truly love animals, they often do not realize that an exotic in captivity has the potential to be more dangerous than an animal in the bush. Animals in the wild have a natural fear of man, which keeps them at a respectful distance. An exotic in a home in which it has been allowed to become spoiled has no such fear and respect. As a result, it resents any intrusion or activity from which it will not benefit.

Even if you truly believe you can overcome the difficulties I've outlined thus far, one final obstacle remains: you. Raising an exotic animal requires professional training and personal commitment from the onset of the relationship. This is a twenty-four-hour-a-day, seven-day-a-week relationship for the life of the animal. Can you honestly see yourself spending the rest of your animal's life together?

Suppose you take on the task of raising an exotic animal, but you don't raise it properly. Sooner or later, it will most likely hurt—or perhaps kill—you or someone close to you (and will then have to be put to sleep or given to a zoo).

Perhaps you've raised the animal with affection training, but you are not prepared to keep the animal for all of what may be a thirty-year life expectancy. This is equally irresponsible. When you have committed to raising an exotic, there should be no turning back. The animal looks upon you as its kin. To give it away because it is becoming too large to keep at home can be traumatic, not just for you, but for the animal as well. An animal that has been trained properly needs constant love and support, given with a "hands-on" approach. To put such an animal in a zoo would be tantamount to putting a close friend who had committed no crime into prison.

※

By now, I hope I've convinced you that having an exotic animal at home is not appropriate for the nonprofessional. However, affection-training techniques, while developed for use with exotic animals, can be adapted for use with domestic animals as well. In fact, these principles are equally effective for raising children—my daughter, Tana, is living proof!

Affection training is made up of four important ingredients: love, patience, understanding, and respect. Each of these elements is critical, and all must be present—no one of them can suffice on its own.

LOVE

Love is the prime ingredient in affection training, and caring is one of the tools used to show that love. Although your life may be extremely busy and centered around your work and family, your animal's life is centered around *you*. After all, he is totally dependent on you: he must wait for you to feed him, clean him, take him for walks . . . everything. His total existence depends on your concern. You are responsible for him full time, for the rest of his life. In return for your caring, you receive the animal's devotion.

Touch is another important way of expressing love. Have you ever ruffled a person's hair or slapped someone on the back, only to have them become indignant? Your not knowing when and where to touch an animal can signal the animal that you are not in tune with him. Your hand should always be an extension of your love. Never use it in a violent way. Use it smoothly and gently. Animals respond quickly and psychically to touch. Through your touch they can read your desires and gauge your sincerity; your touch shows them whether you are a friend or an enemy.

Animals also experience love through your voice. The inflection and volume of your voice are critical in controlling the animal, in making your feelings known to him, and in rewarding him for a deed well done.

Most vocal commands should consist of one-syllable words, such as *come, sit,* and *stay,* which are easier for an animal to recognize than phrases such as "Come here" or "Sit down." The most important word your animal will ever hear is *no.* You should never have to say it twice; if you do, you're not doing your job properly. *No* can save an animal from an accident, injury, or death—or even from hurting another animal.

PATIENCE

The second ingredient in affection training is patience. Many people have difficulty just waiting for a stop light to change or a toaster to pop. Training an animal requires a great deal more patience. Having patience means taking the time to relax. It means not getting upset when the animal you have spent hours training forgets! Also, animals do best when following a routine, which may become boring for you and will therefore require extra patience.

To develop patience in yourself, try learning it from the animal. Animals live in a timeless state; they exist completely in the moment. They're not concerned about what happened yesterday or worried about tomorrow. If you can tap into that timeless space in your animal, you can acquire the patience needed for affection training.

UNDERSTANDING

We humans have been trying to understand the world of animals and their relationship to us for eons. While at first such understanding may seem easy—after all, animals can be depended on to do pretty much the same things at the same time and in the same way—this is *not* what I mean by understanding.

The type of understanding that goes into affection training derives from communication. What are your animal's emotional needs? How does the animal cope with difficult situations?

Truly understanding an animal means knowing the animal as well as he knows himself. This is achieved by caring for him, getting involved in his way of life, and being open to learning about his wants, needs, and stresses. For example, to really understand a bear, you have to "be" like a bear. Swimming with him, brushing his back, wrestling with him, sharing honey and watermelon with him, napping together under a tree—all these can allow you to enter the bear's domain. At some point during this process a door will open. Something will happen. You will *know*.

RESPECT

Respect must be earned. This is true for people, and it is true for animals. When the animal has experienced your love, your patience, and your willingness to be understanding, you will have earned that animal's respect.

Some people confuse the respect that has been earned by fear with the respect earned by love. *They are not the same.* While an animal that is physically abused will do as he's commanded, on the inside he's always looking for a moment to retaliate. Moreover, the animal doesn't really respect the trainer, but the weapon the trainer uses on him.

An animal trained with affection training does as he's asked because he enjoys it, not because he's forced to. Even the rewards he receives (such as a tidbit of food) are used as more of a thank-you than a training device. Many times I've seen an affection-trained animal turn down a reward but continue to perform simply to please his trainer, whom he loves, and who cares for him.

If you honor the first three rules—love, patience, and under-standing—you will automatically receive respect.

✸

The bridge of communication between man and animal crosses an unexplored territory. The techniques I've described above only scratch the surface of affection training. They are therefore meant to be considered merely as guidelines to an intricate pattern of animal behaviorism, not as a complete program for animal training.

7

WHERE HAVE ALL
THE ANIMALS GONE?

Without warning, the week-old storm moved inland. Temperatures dropped into the mid-twenties, and an unusual freezing-cold rain turned into a howling, raging snowstorm, the first in many years in this part of California. The formerly gentle countryside now loomed cold and hostile under its new blanket of crisp white snow.

The fifty-year-old, run-down Spanish hacienda that served as our ranch was nestled in a grove of giant eucalyptus trees at the very top of Mulholland Drive in the Santa Monica Mountains, and it lay directly in the path of the storm. Although on a clear day you could see the crystal-blue water of the Pacific Ocean some 25 miles away, due to the storm's intensity the visibility was now under 100 feet.

Although the exterior of the house was almost foreboding in appearance, the feeling inside was one of warmth and hospitality. All of the sixteen rooms were strangely interlocked: there were doors in the backs of closets, and others behind a mirrored wall. The hub of activity was the massive main room downstairs—approximately fifty feet long and almost thirty feet wide, with an eighteen-foot ceiling. At each end, oak-banistered staircases led up to the second floor. In the center was an enormous walk-in fireplace made of flagstone and mortar brick; its dominance was felt from wherever one stood in the room. Our only sources of heat were this fireplace and six smaller ones spread throughout the house.

Outside, the property sloped gently down to a small valley. An ice-cold creek dodged its way through the groves of oaks and patches of ironwood until it dropped off a rock crevice, cascading down the mountainside like a miniature waterfall. A six-horse barn, complete with a hayloft and outside runs for the horses, dominated the valley.

When we had leased the property, we had built rows of chain-link cages to hold our exotic animals, as well as pipe corrals for the hay-eating stock. The house and grounds were to be home not only to us, but also to dozens of wild animals—lions, tigers, leopards, and chimpanzees, as well as domestic stock such as horses, cows, goats, and pigs.

✺

My team had come together from all parts of the country. Each member was a dedicated animal lover who had heard of my specialized work in the behavioral training of exotic animals. Although some had no professional knowledge of animals, they brought with them something far more important—love. Over time our little group had developed into a family. We cared for one another, worked together, and lived in the big house communal-style. We all shared the belief that what we were doing would ultimately benefit mankind—that by using a hands-on approach in working with wild animals, an approach based on love and respect rather than brutality, we could help to bring about a greater understanding of animals and an appreciation of their value to society.

Ted, my head man and protégé, was good-looking and muscular, with a great personality and a love of nature. Ted's optimism dominated everything. To him, every day was a glorious event; no matter how bad the circumstances might be, Ted always believed that we could overcome the problems.

Joy was the general manager and backbone of the company. Other female staff members included Joy's mother, Ruth; Ma Pud, our cook; and Laura, a promising trainer.

Don, a young teenager, had come to us after having spent

many of his years as a runaway. After much deliberation between his parents (who did not want him) and the judge (who wanted to send him to juvenile hall), Don was legally allowed to stay with us. Although to the outside world he appeared to be a rebel, he was warm and gentle with the people he knew and trusted, and above all with the animals he cared for.

The youngest member of our team was Maria, a thin pixie of a girl. She had come to us one day from up north, alone and depressed, carrying a knapsack bigger than she was. She was looking for a new way of life. Her distrust of people had contributed to her becoming an introvert, and she kept to herself most of the time. From the day she plunked her knapsack down at our front door, I knew that this sensitive and dedicated young woman could benefit deeply from the love and tranquility that the animals had to offer.

Maria loved to sing. One could hear her lilting, childlike tones emanating from her room, from the kitchen, or from the forest. But now, even Maria was silent. Due to the raging storm, which had caught us totally unprepared, it had been five days since we had been able to communicate with the outside world. The electric lines were down, the telephone was dead, and the twisting two-lane road leading up the mountain from Thousand Oaks, seventeen miles away, was impassable. Food for the animals, especially the meat eaters, would soon run out, to say nothing of *our* food supply, which was desperately short. And we had no idea how long the storm would last.

Since it was so large, the house required a tremendous amount of firewood to keep it warm, and we were running low. We needed to bring in a large supply if we were to make it through the storm. Even Ted seemed a bit depressed as he came in from checking on the animals in the compound. "I found an enormous dead tree down the mountainside about 300 yards from the house," I said to perk him up. "We could sure use it for firewood, but it's going to be tough work bringing it up to the house. Do you want to give it a try?"

"Yeah, sure," Ted said with an unusual lack of enthusiasm.

"How is everybody down below?" I asked, knowing that conditions were getting worse by the day.

"We're just holding our own," he said. "Everybody's dry, at least for now—but I've got to tell you, Ralph, it's getting scary."

I put my hand on his shoulder. "I know, but hey—a group like us. . . ."

"I know," Ted interrupted. "It's no problem!"

"No problem" was the team's unofficial slogan. Ted and I both laughed, and as I put on my jacket I yelled, "Whoever wants to help haul a tree for firewood, let's go!"

Affirmative responses were heard throughout the house. We zipped up our parkas and headed out into the blizzard. For three hours, Ted, Maria, Don, Joy, Laura, Ruth, and I pushed and pulled, fell and slid trying to haul that tree up the mountain, but for all our efforts we only gained about a hundred feet.

We plopped on the tree trunk, utterly exhausted. "What now?" Joy asked.

Suddenly I got an idea. "Let's get some horses and a couple of ropes—that'll help." Ted and I headed for the barn and chose the two stallions to ride. Stud was built more like a racing quarter, with sleek lines, long legs, and delicate features, while Son was a roping quarter and, with his thick chest, short legs, and powerful muscles, resembled a bulldozer.

The two "girls," Midnight and Mollie, were left behind, warm and comfortable in the barn.

With ropes tied around the tree and everyone pushing, we threw a loop around the saddle horns and gave a click of the tongue to the horses to pull. And pull they did. They strained into their chest plates, with steam pouring from their nostrils in huge spurts; sometimes they slipped, and at times even fell. But, together with the team, they managed to get the oak up to the back door of the house. I rode Son through the door and into the main room and threw a new loop over the roots of the tree. With all of us pushing, we managed to get the roots up to the edge of the fireplace. Dismounting, I grabbed the roots; everybody followed suit, and we raised that section enough to thrust the whole base of the tree into the huge fireplace.

While the main room was nearly thirty feet wide from the fireplace to the door, the tree was thirty-eight feet long! As a result, a good portion of it stuck out the back door. But we were content with the fact that at least we could have a fire. We knew, too, that the roots would eventually burn down, and we planned to inch the tree into the fireplace until we could close the back door.

After I had put Son in his stall, I walked over to the compound. Zamba was pacing in his cage, anticipating another night of thunder and lightning. He had abhorred thunder ever since he'd been a cub. He jumped up against the chain links, all 9 feet and 528 pounds of him, and looked down at me, begging to be loved. I couldn't resist, so I opened the door and went in to put his leash on. He exploded with joy, leaping and running all over his cage. At my command of "down," he rolled to a stop and lay upside down at my feet, looking up at me with his huge golden eyes. When I reached down to put on his leash, he pulled me down on top of him with his paws and proceeded to give me a rather raspy lick across my face. God, what a great lion, what a great friend!

Zamba loved the snow, taking great delight in jumping into a drift and scattering the snow in all directions. The wind would blow the soft powdery flakes into swirls; like a white curtain, the mist of snow would settle over him. Then, our ghostly-looking lion would high-step majestically, seeming to admire his new white cape.

We arrived at the house covered in snow from the romp. A blazing fire was going, and everybody was huddled around it. I tied Zamba to a special grommet that I had secured to the floor. The leash was long enough to allow him to rest his head on my lap, but not so long that he could get too near the fire. I put a small saucer of milk down for Zamba to slurp up.

Everybody had brought a blanket and pillow and had secured his or her own territory near the tree. Maria, Laura, and Joy had brought some baby animals up from the compound to insure their safety from the cold, and we turned some of them—Jacks, a squirrel monkey; Kabor, a marmoset; Stinky, a skunk; and

Bandit, a raccoon—loose on the tree. Jacks and Kabor, both tiny and delicate, lived together in the nursery. Jacks had beautiful dark eyes, elflike ears, and a long tail that, when not being used for balance, was curled up between his legs and over his shoulder. He would fall asleep holding it like a pillow. Kabor, a bit smaller, had a white tuft of hair sprouting from the top of his head. He could always be found nestled close to Jacks.

Stinky and Bandit were also roommates and clearly cared for each other very much, although their personalities were quite different. Stinky liked to sleep a lot, and Bandit was always waking her up by jumping right in the middle of her back! Stinky would arch her tail at him, not realizing that her scent glands had been removed.

The four little animals scampered up and down the tree, enjoying its many avenues of "hide and seek." Among the branches and along the bark, ants had set out on a long journey to gather what food information they could, sending it back to the colony through the ranks at incredible speed. Some ladybugs were setting up house in a niche of dried leaves and twigs.

Hordes of beetles clambered everywhere, decorated with red, blue, and green patterns of color—some with dots, some with stripes. All were on a mission, and all had a purpose: to escape the advancing flames. The slow-burning wood gave most of them a chance to make it to safety—unfortunately, that meant into the house. We had to step lightly for the next few days, as the multicolored beetles, columns of ants, and even an old daddy longlegs were all scampering for new quarters.

Zamba lay his great head in my lap. I felt a tremble go through his body whenever the lightning flashed, as he waited for the thunder that would follow.

The blaze of the fire cast a cavelike glow in the room; all else was pitch-black. The inner warmth visible in the eyes of the disheveled group told me that this was a special shared moment.

The Bible says that a tree is a symbol of wisdom. So it may be, but it also gives of itself—its strength, its security, and its protection. To touch it was to tune in to the soul of nature, to become one with the infinite.

Joy snuggled down in her comforter. "I feel guilty," she said quietly. "With all the stress and worry, I still feel wonderful, and I don't understand it."

"You feel as the animals do, Joy: as part of a group, not as an individual," I said. "If a person on a crowded street in New York sees a runaway car coming in his direction, he and he alone panics and runs, knocking into others who remain unaware of the impending danger. But if a group of antelope are feeding on the veldt and only one sees a lion approaching, *all* react as one. All run in the same direction without knocking into one another, because they are listening to a universal 'mind.' But man is an individual, and his thoughts are his own.

"What you feel here tonight is that same wonderful sharing that animals have naturally, whether in emergency or tranquility. We are so close to our animals and our love is so strong that we have entered into their dominion. Perhaps someday others, too, will be able to share nature's perfected way, and hopefully will benefit from it before it's too late."

There was a long, heavy silence. Everyone was deep in thought. From a pile of blankets, bodies, and animals came someone's voice: "No problem." Everyone broke up.

Finally we fell asleep. When a chill would awaken us, we would push the tree a little further into the fireplace, where it would blaze anew. We continued this ritual until we could finally close the back door.

In the middle of the night I awoke and walked quietly over to the window. I looked out at a frozen white world. Nothing moved. A bright moon lit up the countryside with an eerie glow. There were no clouds, nothing to identify the movement of life. I felt moved by secretly watching nature sleep.

I turned toward the fire, where the tree loomed as mother protector. Everyone was asleep: territories ignored, animals cuddled against the warmth of the tree. Zamba was curled up, kitten-like. The hot bright coals threw light against the tree branches and reflected them against the ceiling. I hurried back to the warmth of Zamba and snuggled up under his mane, content.

By dawn the storm started to rage again. Food supplies were

getting critically low. We were feeding 500 pounds of meat per day just to the big cats—the lions, tigers, and leopards—and tons of alfalfa and oat hay went to the hoofed stock.

I was deep in thought, computing how to ration the food among the animals, when I heard someone scream.

Screams of any kind give one a chilling sensation, but a scream on a wild-animal ranch is bloodcurdling. Was something or somebody being killed? Many times in my life I've had to pull someone from a horrible situation and hearing that scream sent my adrenaline racing.

I leaped to the window. In the snow-covered valley by the horse barn, I saw a small human figure running, screaming, and falling in the heavy snow. I raced out the door and slipped and slid the quarter-mile distance to the barn.

It was Maria. When I got to her, she was hysterical. She threw her arms around me, crying and shaking. I wiped the snow from her face and tried to calm her down as best as I could. I half-carried her back to the horse barn, from where, according to her tracks, she had just come.

The stench of horses and hay assaulted me as we piled inside. And then I saw them: lying all around—some dead and some dying—were horses. I stood there, stunned. *What? How?* It couldn't have been the cold—the barn was warm enough.

I ran to Stud, to Molly, to Midnight—all the horses that had helped me to build the ranch, horses that I had known for a long time and that, like all the other animals, had become a part of our family.

Maria had gone over to Midnight, her favorite, whom she had always been seen riding, preening, and grooming. Midnight was lying flat out, every other breath a work of labor. Together we tried to get her to stand, but try as we might to help her, she just couldn't make it. The door burst open and Joy, Ted, Laura, and Don poured in. Their faces all registered the sudden shock I had felt just moments before. Each went to his or her favorite horse and pleaded with it to get up: "Thatta boy." "Come on, you can do it!" Three or four of us would all pitch in as one. Pulling, hauling, bracing with our backs, we would finally get one animal to stand for a moment, only to have it topple over again.

We fetched blankets and lanterns and built a small fire. I wracked my brain to figure out what had happened. They had been kept warm enough; the only thing I could think of was food poisoning. I walked over to the hay, and then I saw it. Mold! Apparently, the rain and snow had caught the edge of the hay, and mold had formed. But why this? I had seen horses eat moldy hay before, but they hadn't *died* from it!

I decided to send Ted on a mission to find out whether the hay was truly bad, and also to bring back dearly needed supplies. I would stay at the ranch, since I was best equipped to handle the situation.

I called the group together. Except for Maria, who wouldn't leave Midnight, we all huddled near the fire.

"Look, Ted, it's up to you, buddy. The snow here has stopped, at least for now. It may be the only chance we've got to get you down."

"I don't mind going," he said, "but I don't think Old Betsy can make it up the driveway to the main road. The tires will just spin out."

Don, who rarely spoke, suggested that we modify the car chains to fit with the truck chains for added traction.

Laura suggested we could use Son. "He didn't eat whatever made the others sick, so he's fine. Use him to help pull the truck out to the main road. It's all downhill from there."

"Okay," I said, "but Ted, if we get you up and over the driveway, you're on your own for seventeen miles downhill on a road you probably won't even be able to see," I said.

"No problem," Ted answered with a chuckle.

A light snow had started to fall as Ted climbed into the truck. He turned her engine over; she sputtered, then jumped and roared into action.

I jumped on Son's back, while Don tied a rope to the truck's bumper. I tied the other end to the saddlehorn. Meanwhile the girls had lined the road ahead with brush and twigs. The double chains looked awkward, but strong. I gave the signal, the motor roared, Son pulled, everybody pushed, and off Old Betsy went, backfiring, slipping and sliding, chains biting into the wet mush. Before we knew it, Ted was over the rise and onto what we believed was the road. I unhitched the rope from the bumper. With a wave and a honk, Ted was off, the truck spinning sideways, weaving and sliding, down the mountain, until he disappeared around the mountainside. How he could ever make it down the hill, let alone back up? It was an insane plan, but we had no other options.

The storm had picked up, and the snow and wind had increased to gale force. By the time we reached the house, it was as though the powers above had held the storm back to give Ted a chance. I tried not to think of the consequences if he didn't make it.

We set to work making the remaining horses as comfortable as possible. Two were dead. The stud was going fast. I left Maria and Don to tend to the horses' needs, and the rest of us went out to feed, bed down, and water the other animals. We separated the bad hay from the good. The meat had run out, so to feed the big cats we had to kill laying chickens from the roost. Feeding a two- or three-pound chicken to a lion is like feeding an apple to an elephant, but at least it was something. Their stomachs wouldn't be totally empty that night.

When the sun set that evening on the cold, isolated valley, Maria refused to come up to the house, insisting on staying with Midnight. I left her enough wood to keep a fire going all night.

Dawn broke cold and gray. I threw on an old army jacket and headed outside. The crunch of the snow was all that I heard on the walk to the barn.

The night's snowfall had caused drifts to pile up around the barn door, but since the snow was fresh and soft it yielded to my push. I stepped quietly in, prepared for the worst. The fire in the barn had gone out, and everything was still. My eyes skipped from one form to another. Was that a sign of life? A tremble? Some of the horses lay in the shadows, others with the beam of the morning sun stretched across their faces. Odd that we die with our eyes open—cold, glazed eyes stared at me from everywhere.

I looked for Midnight. She was lying near the burned-out fire, her fuzzy black fur cold and damp. Maria was sleeping nestled in Midnight's forelegs. Her arm was cocked up over the animal's neck; one hand was hidden in the mane as though she had gone to sleep stroking it. I touched Midnight—her body was cold and hard. My God, she was dead! To awaken Maria to this . . . had Midnight died before Maria fell asleep, or after?

To be in love with nature and so attached to her animals— how it hurts when they go; how it tears at your guts! I knelt down and brushed the hair from Maria's eyes. She stirred. I shook her gently, and she awoke. Then I knew. Midnight had died during the night in her arms, for Maria's slowly opening eyes were shimmering with tears. I held her as she wept softly, her body cold and shaking. All around me there was not a single movement. They were *all* dead.

✳

It had been three days since Ted had left. A horn sounded, a *car* horn! Rushing outside, we were just in time to see Ted coming over the ridge, honking the horn and skidding all the way. He had made it!

The truck was piled high with equipment, food supplies, and medicine. The vet had analyzed the mold and found it to be botulism, one of the most deadly of all poisons. Nothing could have helped the horses. We could feed the rest of the good hay to the other livestock.

Ted had brought as much meat as the truck would hold— possibly a few days' supply, and that night everybody feasted! After dinner, Ted took me aside. "I almost didn't make it," he said. "Came close to going over many times. But look, Ralph, Dr. Freeman, well . . . he realizes the problem we're having, and, well . . . while I was in his office I heard on the news that there was no sign of the storm letting up." Ted put his head down.

"What are you trying to tell me, Ted?" I asked. "Just say it."

Ted adjusted his Western hat, pulling it low over his forehead. "The cats aren't going to make it, Ralph, unless. . . ."

"Unless what?!"

"Unless we feed the horse meat to them."

"My God, man, what are you saying? Feed them Molly and

69

Stud and Midnight? You're crazy! We'll find another way," I said, and walked off.

Ted yelled after me, "Doc said the meat won't hurt them—just don't feed them the insides!"

Deep down, Ted knew—as I too came to realize—that there was no other way.

The next few days were murderously cold and wet. The situation on the ranch became desperate. Again Ted approached me about the horse meat, and I called a meeting by the fire. I told the group what the vet had suggested. In the flickering firelight I could see the dejected faces, the lowered eyes. Yet everyone understood, particularly after Maria raised her head and said, "Midnight is long gone from that cold, dead body lying down there in the barn, and I'm sure she would agree that if it's to help her buddies, her animal friends, then it's . . . well . . . okay."

I had all of the knives sharpened, and Ted, Don, and I were preparing to leave, when the girls came up to us. They were dressed in boots, heavy jackets, wool scarves, and gloves. They were going to help. Even Maria—so tiny—was not about to be talked out of it.

I used the old truck to pull some of the carcasses out of the barn. Each person went to work. Maria would let no one help her. The job was tremendous for a big man, let alone for a very little lady. By evening, snow had started to fall again. Everyone else had finished, and only Maria and I were left in the barn. I pretended to be doing some work around the barn, not wanting to leave.

Maria looked up at me, her tears like small white snowflakes on her cheeks.

"Ralph," she said, in a voice barely audible against the wind, "could I . . . ?" She wiped her eyes against the sleeve of her coat. I could tell that what she had to say was difficult for her. "I mean, if the weather is okay, could I ride Son tomorrow?"

I couldn't hide my tears, but they were tears of joy. I knew then that Maria was going to make it. "Sure, honey," I said, "if the weather is okay." A slight move of her lip and chin said "thank you," and she went back to her chore.

Turning, I started up the snow-covered hill. The snowflakes had become larger and were falling thicker and faster. A slight wisp of warm breeze caught me off guard—dry wind that comes in from the desert and sweeps down across the valley. I knew that the worst was over.

Partway up I stopped as I heard Maria singing, and I turned and looked back. She was sitting inside the large cavity of Midnight, quietly cutting as the light from a small candle flickered against the rib walls, the collar of her coat pulled way up around her neck. The horse's blood mingled with the snow, and little rivulets of red wound their way down the white mountainside. The noise of the knife softly echoed in the valley. As I turned to go, I heard Maria sobbing as she quietly sang a favorite tune. I noticed she had changed the words:

> *Where have all the animals gone?*
> *Long time passing . . .*
> *Where have all the animals gone?*
> *Long time ago . . .*
> *Where have all the animals gone?*
> *Gone to graveyards, every one.*
> *When will we ever learn,*
> *When will we ever learn?*

PART III

"NO PROBLEM"

When you're young, or hungry, or trying to prove yourself, nothing *seems impossible.*

To die? Impossible! To be hurt? Unthinkable!

When the studio would call asking me to kiss a cobra, fall off a charging elephant, or fight with a leopard, my answer was always the same: "No problem." Did I have a lion that could be ridden by a child? "No problem." What about an orangutan that could drive? "No problem." What about an elephant that would let a mouse climb on his trunk? "No problem."

It never occurred to me that I might get hurt; I was simply too busy to think about it. I needed the money and the experience, and above all, I wanted to show everybody that I could do it. "Early ego," I call it. Anyway, I'd always been a risk-taker.

As I grew older, I traded some of that ego for wisdom. It became clear to me that taking risks could be dangerous, even fatal.

8

THE HUG OF DEATH

"You want me to do *what?*" I asked the caller on the telephone. "Yes, that's what I thought you said—you want me to dress as a woman and wrestle a giant python. Yes, I'm a stuntman, and yes, I do work with reptiles. But that's not what bothers me. It's the dressing as a woman. . . .

"Uh-huh, yes, well, her being cute and having a great body does not help the matter one single bit. Look, I have to think about this. I'll call you tomorrow, George."

So much for the glamour of Hollywood. I had been doing stunts with animals—some wild, some domestic—for a number of years. I had wrestled tigers and lions, fought bears, and handled cobras and rattlesnakes. This was my life, and I thoroughly enjoyed it. But this bit about dressing as a woman threw me a curve.

The next day, I called George and asked him about as many details of the stunt job as I could. It appeared that the filmmakers wanted the largest snake available to be put up in a tree, from where it would attack a "jungle girl" as she passed beneath it. Once the snake was around her neck, the "girl" was to struggle with it until her "savior," a white hunter, appeared and rescued her by pulling the snake off. In spite of the teasing I knew I would get, I reluctantly said yes. Work, after all, was work.

The snake I chose was one of the largest, heaviest, and, above all, *meanest* reptiles around. She was the only snake I have ever known that seemed more like a warm-blooded mammal than a cold-blooded reptile. Her name was Consuela. She was a 26-foot,

255-pound, reticulated python who hated people and would try to do them in any chance she got.

Consuela, naturally, had no friends. She considered everything alive to be either food or an enemy. She was owned by a professional artist friend of mine who had used her as a model for many of his sculptures. Whenever I had asked him in the past if I could use his snake for a film or a TV spot, he had always said no. He believed she was too dangerous to handle, and that someone would be likely to get hurt. But this time, after a bit of persuasion, he allowed me to use her, as long as he could be there as one of the handlers. I agreed, and we decided to meet to discuss the details of the fight.

The next evening, as arranged, I let myself into his dimly lit studio for our meeting. Around me stood various pieces of African and Indian sculpture. The small pieces were sitting on pedestals; the larger ones, which stood five or six feet tall, rested on slabs of marble. Spotlights hung from the ceiling in every conceivable angle to catch the sculptures at their best. Most pieces were of black ebony that my friend had brought back from a visit to the Makonde tribe in East Africa. They depicted the traditional and surrealistic world of that little-known and diminishing culture. With their huge, limpid eyes, elongated arms and legs, and lips curled in pain or pleasure, the sculptures threw grotesque shadows across the room. Among the art pieces, four or five in particular stood out: these were giant snakes, some in deadly, coiled positions, ready to attack, others expressing the sheer beauty of the creature's form—its symmetrical body lying upon itself, resting on its own defenses, the giant head lording over the mountains and valleys of coils.

However, the work that impressed me most of all was a huge, freestanding sculpture of an African man caught in the massive coils of an enormous snake. The coils around his neck caused his eyes to bulge beyond the sockets. His body had lost all of its normal shape and now conformed to the desires of the coils. His arms and legs lay swollen and limp; the rest of his body had disappeared beneath roll upon roll of coiled death. The snake's head lay inches from the man's face. It was watching him die, waiting to begin engulfing him, head first. The man's face expressed sheer terror, the realization of the inevitable. I felt a cold shudder go through my body.

I carefully edged my way through the gallery. A bright, piercing light could be seen coming from a back room, and I headed through the "tribes" to its source. On the floor in the middle of the room was a huge, square wooden box. One side was made of heavy thick glass, and from it came the source of light. Lying inside the box was Consuela. Her massive frame nearly filled the box.

Mishka rose from the shadows. We exchanged the usual greetings, and he offered me a seat in front of what he called "the television." I guess the box did resemble a TV set, in a way, but the type of drama that was about to unfold in it would surely have no sponsors.

A friend of Mishka's brought in a carrying case filled with two dozen rats. I noticed that all the rats were fully grown and probably weighed about one pound each. All were the domestically raised white-and-black laboratory animals that I had often seen before. Heat plays an important part in the snake's digestive system, so Mishka raised the thermostat level in the cage to the proper degree. While waiting for the temperature to rise, we began to discuss the moral issue of feeding live animals to snakes.

Most snakes eat only live rodents. This was nature's way, and it wasn't up to us to change it. Still, we wondered, weren't we playing God when we picked out which rats were to die and which were to be spared for yet another night? Of course, it isn't any different down in the stockyards, where man kills steers, lambs, goats, chickens, and pigs for human consumption.

When the proper temperature had been reached, Mishka picked up the box of rats. He reminded me that we should keep our movements to a minimum, although the bright light in the cage and the darkness outside it prevented most movement from being seen by the snake. I was amazed when Mishka then opened the cage's top door and dumped the whole two dozen rats onto Consuela! I had been expecting him to feed them to her one at a time. The rats landed in different positions and areas all over

Consuela's body, then began to sniff and crawl around, seemingly not the least bit concerned about their hostess.

My eyes were riveted to Consuela. The standard approach a snake would take under these conditions would be to tighten its neck muscles into an "S" position and focus in on one particular rat. It would then strike and constrict the animal until it stopped breathing, then devour it, head first.

Not so with Consuela. I watched as she began to undulate her coils. Every section of her body was moving, each in its own direction. Occasionally, her tongue would slither out, picking up any vibrations. Her eyes moved constantly as she watched her victims keenly. I couldn't figure out why she didn't strike. She could have had any rat she chose. My first thought was that she was used to eating much bigger food, like rabbits, and so perhaps felt that rats weren't worth the effort.

Meanwhile, her body had moved itself into an interesting and baffling form. Consuela's main body was spread in a loose circle around the enclosure, and two arm-size coils lay parallel across the box from its furthest point up to her head. She lay perfectly still. Then, as if a button had been pushed, her body began to move in a meticulous and strange way. Wherever she engaged a rat between her coils and the wall of the cage, she forcefully pinned it there, squeezing it until all its breath stopped. Then the coil relaxed. This was happening simultaneously all over the cage. Seven or eight rats were being squeezed to death at one time, and she hadn't even opened her mouth once to strike. Her attitude was that of a sloth. The rats were incidental to her. Why should she bother herself with a highly intense strike, when all she had to do was wait until a rat moved between her and a hard spot, and . . . *gotcha?*

The most ingenious part was yet to come. While all these individual kills were happening, other coils were now coming into place. As each rat was dealt with, it was put in the middle of the two long parallel coils. These started to move, carrying the rat along, as if on a conveyor belt, heading directly for her mouth. Sometimes, four or five rats at a time could be seen moving along, heading straight into Consuela's gaping jaws. As they approached, she opened her mouth, and one by one each rat was grasped and sent on its way down her juicy pink throat.

Not once in the entire feeding did she strike or show any other outward sign of aggression. This lady was clever. She knew how to get the job done quickly and efficiently. She knew that striking and killing each rat individually would take a long time and a lot of energy. In less than an hour's time, all two dozen rats had disappeared down her throat. Even though the rats together weighed about twenty-four pounds, they didn't even raise a bulge in her stomach. How massive she was! I'm sure that in the wild she could easily have killed and consumed animals weighing fifty or sixty pounds.

This was the monster I was to wrestle. She outweighed me by a hundred pounds, and she had the strength of twenty men. I'd need to use all I'd ever learned—with some luck thrown in—to tangle with her and come out alive.

Mishka and I talked late into the evening about our plan, while Consuela lay in the cage with her head resting on her coils. Her body, with its reticulated pattern of color and design, glistened an iridescent light blue. Maybe she was asleep, maybe not. You can't tell with snakes, since they have no eyelids. She just gazed off into her primal world, always ready—eyes darting, searching for her next meal. Only when the cage lights were turned off could she truly sleep, with the dark serving as closed eyelids for her. But if one could see her eyes close up in the pitch black, I'm sure they would still be twitching, searching, looking for another rat.

✹

On the day of the shoot, I arrived at the movie studio around six in the morning. With me were three of my best men. I had sent the others over to Mishka's to assist in loading Consuela and the heavy cage.

The director was a nice chap. We spent an hour going over exactly what he wanted. I told him that snakes, like many exotic animals, are unpredictable, and that I would do the best I could.

He accepted that, and he then brought up another possibility. He had asked during our previous conversation how we would manage to keep the snake from biting me. I explained that we would put a special snakeskin muzzle over Consuela's mouth that would match her color and so would not be visible. The coils would be enough to worry about—I didn't need the added fear of 200 needle-like teeth trying to bite me. The director lowered his head and asked, his voice hesitating, "Do you ever wrestle snakes without a muzzle?"

"Well, yes, sometimes, if I feel I can control the situation."

"To see the gaping mouth and all those teeth would be sensational," he said, almost talking to himself. "What do you think? Any chance?"

As a director, he had a right to ask. And as a stuntman, I had the right to reject.

"I'll pay triple," he said, luring me. "I know the risk is there, but you have a lot of help, and I'll cut the camera whenever you say."

"My God, man, do you realize that I can't hold the weight of that snake *and* her head for more than a fleeting moment? Don't you have any idea how powerful she is?" But my common sense was weighing against one hell of a lot of money. My company had been in tough financial straits for the last six months, and what with mortgage payments, cage repairs, veterinarian bills, feed costs, etcetera, there just hadn't been enough to go around.

Wait a minute, I thought to myself. This is crazy! It's not worth it.

The director got up and dusted off his pants. "Think about it!" he said, and left.

In the meantime, I met the actress, a buxom, dark-haired beauty. She was dressed in a complete "jungle safari" outfit from top to bottom, straight out of Saks Fifth Avenue. In all my trips to Africa I have never once seen the safari outfits depicted in Hollywood movies.

My next stop was wardrobe. They went to work on me, cinching my waist, putting on falsies, cutting and measuring.

Two hours later I walked out, looking incredibly like the actress. But there was more to come. After wardrobe came the hair department, where I was fitted with a wig. Finally, there was something I hadn't counted on, which truly made me almost an exact double. The studio had made a full rubber mold of the actress's face, and when this mask was slipped on me and makeup applied, there was no doubt—I *was* the actress!

Finally, Mishka and the men arrived with Consuela. I noticed she was cool and calm, not the least bit riled by the trip. The prop man brought over the snakeskin muzzle. I took a deep breath and said, "Thanks, but no thanks. Take it back."

Mishka froze. "Are you *crazy,* Ralph? The bitch will kill you!" He grabbed the muzzle from the prop man. "Come on, don't joke around," he said.

"It's no joke, Mishka. I've decided to give it a try."

"What did he do? Offer you the cash register? Ralph, it's just not worth the risk."

"I appreciate your concern," I told him, "but I figure the whole fight can't last three minutes. If I'm careful and quick, and I watch the neck coil, it can work."

Mishka studied my face for a long time. He knew that if I were even considering taking the risk, I must *really* need the money.

Mishka begrudgingly handed the muzzle back to the prop man. "It's your life—at least, let's hope so. What can *I* do to help keep you alive?"

I gathered my men together and, with Mishka, we set our plan. The studio had constructed a platform up in the trees overlooking the branch on which Consuela was to lie. It was strong enough to support the cage and four men. Mishka and I would slip a black hood over Consuela's head to keep her calm until we had her in position. When the director yelled "Ready," we would quickly muscle her out of the box and lay her on the thick branch. Then I would stand under the branch and reach up, holding the snake's hooded head. At the call for "Action," one of my trainers would jerk the hood off, and the rest would be history. We went over the standard cues: if I raised one finger off the coils, it meant I had one minute of breathing left; two fingers meant I was okay;

and three fingers meant that there was an emergency and I needed help.

I received hugs for good luck from both the actress and the director. The assistant director yelled, "Quiet on the set!" Four of my men were stationed on top of the platform, ready to haul the hooded Consuela out. I stationed myself directly beneath the tree branch. Three of my men were standing near the camera. I took a couple of long breaths to get some oxygen into my blood, then I gave the signal that I was ready.

My men up on the platform acted as one, knowing that if they hesitated with Consuela for too long a period, she could become violent with them and ruin the whole scene. They raised the cage's heavy top door, and then eight hands reached in together: two for the head, four for the middle section, and two for the lower section and tail. Even for four men she was a heavy load. They draped her on the limb and handed me the hooded head. As the director yelled "Action!" a trainer pulled the string, and the hood was off.

I was holding Consuela with both of my hands around her neck, and I felt a jolt of energy shoot through her body. It was so strong that it nearly dislodged my hands. I looked down just in time to see her elliptical eyes shoot a glance at me. Without hesitating, she struck straight for my face, her mouth wide open. She could easily have engulfed my entire head. The strike threw me up against the tree, and instantly her coils slithered down the trunk across my shoulders, chest, and waist.

Her weight was phenomenal. I could hold my ground as long as she stayed on my body, but if she swung her head out or arched some of her coils, that forty or fifty pounds could cause me to lose my balance and fall. I could hear voices yelling, but because of the mask I couldn't distinguish them or make out what they were saying. Consuela gradually slid her entire body over me. The pressure of her coils lying around my shoulders was excruciating. She was so big that just a single massive coil around my neck reached to the top of my head.

Then she started to constrict.

I knew that if I kept my chin tucked in and down, it would

protect my throat and give me a couple of extra minutes. But Consuela wasted no time, and as her coils encircled my chin I knew from the building pressure that the tightening coil would eventually slip off my chin onto my throat. I figured I had about a minute of breath left, so I prepared to give the one-finger signal.

That's when it happened. In the struggle, I jerked my head to the side as the snake was constricting her coils in the opposite direction. This caused the sweaty rubber mask to be pulled around on my face. Instantly, I couldn't see, I couldn't hear, I couldn't speak, and, worst of all, I couldn't *breathe!* The wall of rubber that was the side of the mask was now directly across the front of my face, and Consuela's massive midsection was squeezing it against me. I hadn't had time to take a breath or to signal for help. She had me, and she knew it.

I didn't dare to release the snake's head, but I knew that if I didn't try to push the coil away from my face I would suffocate. I tried to inhale some air, but the rubber mask was being held so tightly against my mouth that I couldn't even exhale. My equilibrium started to go and I fell to the ground, still holding Consuela's head. I could feel her mouth gape open, trying to reach me. Why wasn't anyone coming to help me? Why didn't they come in and take her off of me? Oh, my God! Of course— *the mask!* They couldn't see me! The mask was hiding all my emotions. They didn't know. I couldn't scream, nor could I give the emergency signal, so they must have thought I was all right.

I remember thinking that a python feels your heartbeat through its delicate underbody. The stronger the heart beats in its fight to pump the blood, the tighter the snake coils; only when the heart stops do the coils relax. With this creature, there is no such thing as playing dead. The last thing I remember of my scene with Consuela is having Mishka's sculpture of the dying man flash across my mind as the noise of my heart beating became louder and louder. Then, nothing.

Everyone watching thought it was an incredible fight—the struggle, the snake's gaping mouth, and, finally, the fall to the ground. The cameras were rolling, and the director was ecstatic. Finally, as my unconscious body relaxed, I let the giant head go.

Consuela arched up high, her head five feet off the ground; her neck was coiled like a steel spring, and her tongue was flickering. My men, sensing a problem, started to move in and were met head-on by a seven-foot strike, which only narrowly missed them. I was being killed by Consuela, and as far as she was concerned, that was that—she wasn't going to let anyone else have me.

One man tried to get her attention, while another sneaked behind her, only to barely miss being impaled on those needlelike teeth. My head trainer, Jim, a big fellow, knew that time was running out. He threw his arms up across his face and charged directly at Consuela, meeting her head-on. Her jaws opened. She caught him flat on his stomach and clenched down on his midsection. He let out a scream and grabbed her neck, but that moment gave the other trainers time to rush in and pull the coils from my body.

I awoke hours later in a hospital bed. It took me forever to realize where I was. I couldn't feel my body; the circulation had been stopped for so long that the blood was still fighting its way through. A giant black-and-blue mark a foot-and-a-half wide circled my chest and back and went over my shoulder, but I was alive. I managed to look across at the bed next to me. Lying in it was the fellow who had saved my life by throwing himself in front of the snake. His belly was exposed, and the whole area was black and blue, and bloody; on it was a giant circle of teeth. With a pair of tweezers, a nurse was pulling out, one by one, each of the snake's teeth that had broken off in his body.

I heard a voice—it was Mishka. "Hey, buddy, welcome back. Everybody wishes you well."

He put a huge get-well card in front of me and showed me all the signatures. In the middle was a caricature of Consuela and me: Consuela had two X's for eyes, and her tongue was hanging out. I was standing above her, with my fists clenched over my head. In the corner of the cartoon was my head trainer, with a red ribbon around his belly. I attempted to smile, and I remember Mishka's saying something about having Consuela and me model for his next sculpture just before I drifted off into blissful sleep.

9

LIONHEARTED

Traffic on the Hollywood Freeway that August morning was heavy with commuters on their way to work. Many were driving with one pinky wrapped tightly around the steering wheel, while they balanced a cup of coffee in one hand and a doughnut in the other.

It was already hot at nine o'clock, heading for a day of hundred-degree-plus heat. A movie studio needed an African lion for a jungle scene by eleven o'clock. Usually we hauled lions in the back of the station wagon, but Tammy—a gorgeous, 350-pound, cream-and-tawny-colored lioness—had a bad habit of rubbing herself raw against the seats. To prevent this, we had put her in the trailer, which was specially designed to house anything weighing up to 600 pounds. Across the top was heavy welded wire, with the back and sides having a special tongue-and-groove wood. The trailer's front housed all the tack needed for the job. We were in no particular hurry and hugged the right side of the road.

Tammy was our most beautiful African lioness, with massive golden eyes in a classic, broad-set head. Although she weighed as much as a young male, she had a very graceful body. Tammy kept herself sparkling clean, and she was always looking for a hug or a kiss from anyone on the ranch.

As our freeway joined the Santa Ana Freeway, we were automatically merged into the fast lane on the left. I was driving, and alongside me sat Frank, my chief trainer and ranch manager at the time. Frank was one of the best. He was a short, stocky man possessed of both great strength and gentleness—a rare, and very useful, combination in our business. I put on my right signal as I attempted to move back over to the slower, far-right lane, but the other drivers were in worlds of their own. They saw and heard nothing other than that which would get them to their destinations as quickly as possible. Giving up, I picked up our speed to match that of the traffic.

Suddenly, the trailer hitch broke! I felt it first as a quiver in the steering wheel. Then the car started to veer. I shot a look into the rearview mirror, and what I saw made my skin crawl. The tongue of the trailer had dropped down to the pavement, so that the trailer was now riding on a tiny metal wheel meant only for jockeying it around—not for driving on. The chain was still attached to the station wagon. When the trailer edged over too far, the chain would whip it back; then it would rebound to the other side, only to be thrown back again. I took my foot off the gas gradually, hoping that this would slow the trailer down. I knew it was only a matter of time before either the chain or the little wheel would break. I hated to think what might happen then.

When the cars around us saw the problem, they raced away, but others quickly filled their void. I smelled burning rubber and saw sparks flying from under the back of the vehicle. I carefully applied the brakes, steadily decreasing my speed.

Then it happened! Either the chain had caught under the tongue of the trailer, or the small wheel had broken. In any case, the trailer's tongue hit the asphalt and dug in.

The sight that greeted me in the mirror paralyzed me with fear. The trailer was in midair and on its way over, in a complete flip. It stayed in midair for what seemed like minutes before it came pinwheeling down, breaking against the wagon. The impact caused me to look ahead quickly enough to prevent us from rolling. It was over in a few seconds.

I pulled to an abrupt stop. Cars were honking, tires screeching. A quick look told me that there hadn't been any collisions. The trailer lay on its side in the fast lane with its wheels spinning, a tire ripped off. It was smoking, the wooden sides were a shambles, and the back door was broken open.

Oh, my God, I thought. *Tammy!!*

Frank and I scrambled out of the car and looked back at the wreckage. We couldn't believe what we saw: there was Tammy, bleeding and bewildered, staggering in the fast lane. Panic-stricken, she was looking straight into four lanes of traffic. Anything could send her directly into it—and to sure death.

"Tammy! Tammy!" I yelled. She stopped moving for a moment. "Tammy, girl . . . come on, baby." Walking again, she was wobbling, weaving into traffic. "Tammy, this way. I'm over here." She looked my way, and then I saw her face. Blood had run into her eyes, and she couldn't see clearly! With all the road noise, it was difficult for her to tell where I was. I moved toward her. "Come on, over here!"

If ever affection training would pay off, this was the time. If Tammy trusted me or cared enough, she would come—if not, she would revert to what any other lion would do, and panic.

"Thatta girl—come on!" I was perhaps fifty feet from her. Frank had circled out into traffic to reroute it away from us, using hand signals only; he was afraid to speak or yell, for fear of confusing Tammy. I was getting closer. Then, with recognition on her face, Tammy started toward me. Cars had stopped, and people were watching in disbelief: a bloody lion on the freeway, walking toward a man.

I slid off my belt, ready to use it as a collar (something I'd done many times before). "Thatta girl, just a little bit further," I said, speaking softly.

Tammy was now "chuffing" at me, making the small, throaty sound that lions make when they recognize or rub up against someone they care for. A lump was forming in my throat. Here was this "blind" lion on the freeway, battered and nearly unconscious, limping toward the sound of my voice. To this day, I have never been more proud of our affection training.

I knelt down as she came to me. When she touched me, she bowled me over with licks, kisses, and hugs. She wiped her bloody head against me, rubbing her eyes clear so she could see. I wrapped the belt around her neck, and together we walked—or, rather, I walked, she staggered—back to the station wagon. I opened the back door, and she jumped onto the seat, lay down, and began licking her wounds. Tammy was safe. It was only then that I heard the horns, the cars starting up, and the scattered applause from the onlookers.

Later, at the veterinary hospital, Tammy's gashes and broken ribs were mended. No one knows how she came through that horrible event so well. Maybe it's because she is an exotic animal, far stronger than her domestic counterparts—or perhaps it's because she was brought up in a way that teaches a relaxed form of life in which fear and panic are not encouraged to prevail. Maybe, when that precise instant between life and death appeared, she chose to relax and roll with the punches rather than fight them. At least, I like to think so.

10

FORBEARANCE

In the movies and on television, the "big four" animals that worked the most were chimps, lions, bears, and elephants. While my stock of animals in the seventies was still not very large, it did include Judy the chimp, Serang the tiger, and Zamba the lion. It was time to find a bear—with no money down. Although our animals were in great shape, we ourselves were barely surviving. Every so often we had to take in our belts a notch.

We had to fight hard to get every job. Our biggest competitor at that time was the World Jungle compound (which would be known later as Jungle Land). It was a large, sprawling company in the Los Angeles suburb of Thousand Oaks. It housed more animals and employed a fair number of trainers. Our advantage was our affection training. Our "love, patience, and understanding with respect" program was in direct opposition to the traditional, "circus-style" program.

Despite the differences in approach, World Jungle had had such greats as Mabel Stark and Mel Coontz on the staff. Both were exceptionally fine trainers, and in the past they had been the backbone of the wild-animal movie industry. Mabel was in her eighties when, working her beloved Jungle Land tigers in the arena one day, she received the news that she was to be let go. She was getting "too old" and was therefore a "great risk." It wasn't long after that that they found her body—losing her "babies" had apparently been too much for her.

Mel was a practical joker. He was always allowing trained animals to run free and scare people. He'd let his lion Jackie lick his forehead and arm until blood was drawn, and then he'd insist that he was being attacked.

I was at World Jungle, assisting Mel with some work, when I learned of a man who wanted to sell a bear that had done extensive work in the movies. The man, Bill Ruskin, lived on a small ranch at the western end of the San Fernando Valley. The ranch was dominated by a big fenced-in yard, which contained a large-antlered deer. Behind the small frame house was a chain-link cage that housed "Pal," the bear.

Bill was a strange man, tall and lanky, with exceptionally large ears and a prominent Adam's apple. He always wore a Western tie and a large-brimmed Western hat. At our first meeting, I found him with his midsection bandaged. He was limping badly.

"Now I see why you want to get rid of your bear," I said.

"No, no, nothing like that!" he explained. "The deer did it. Had him for years, tame as a puppy. Then, when I entered his pen, he charged and pinned me up against the fence. Sunk a couple of those antler points into my belly. He wouldn't let up. I must've been there a good twenty minutes, screaming my head off for someone to help me. Thank goodness my neighbor came by! He grabbed the hose and squirted water into the deer's face until, I guess, he couldn't breathe. In any case, he let me go. I found out later he was in season for rutting."

As we walked over to the bear cage, Ruskin told me about Pal. "He's a strange one, Ralph, but if you're up to it, he'll make a good bear."

Pal was an American black bear, weighing some 500 pounds and standing close to seven feet tall on his hind legs. He had some age on him, maybe twenty-five years. For most of his life he had done studio work, which had clearly worn on him. Pal had been trained by the reward system: work, and you get a treat. The problem was that after Pal was full, nothing could induce him to move. Someone had taken a two-by-four to him to "entice" him to perform; hence his bad attitude—belligerent and abusive.

Ruskin removed the heavy chain that was clipped to the cage, unlocked the door, and put the chain around the bear's neck. Pal ambled out, making a grunting sound. I stood back, respectful of an animal not known to me (and vice-versa).

We then walked toward the back of the property, to a large and fairly open area, with only a few bushes and some rocks. I was surprised to see Ruskin take the chain off Pal's neck.

"Look, Ralph, you seem like a nice kid, so I'm going to level with you," he said. "It takes a lot of guts to work with old Pal. Let me show you how I control him. If I swing my left arm, he'll walk left. If I swing my right arm, he'll walk right. I don't touch or pet him. And Pal will not take any orders from anyone who doesn't pass his test."

"I have to pass *his* test? You're joking!"

"No joke. You see, unless Pal respects you, he won't allow you to command him. He was brought up with a firm hand. Many years ago, Pal refused an order to come when called, and his owner was unmerciful. Pal never forgot that, and when he got older and bigger and stronger, if somebody he didn't respect yelled for him to do something—*anything*—he'd attack. He figured he was going to be beaten, and he wasn't about to let that happen again.

"A friend of the owner's used to feed and care for Pal, and one day he mistakenly ordered him to come. Pal charged. The keeper stood still, and the bear didn't bite him—probably because he knew him. In any case, it did set a precedent. So now all he does is challenge you. If you stand still, he won't attack. But if you run, well—let's just say it's better if you stand still!"

Strange bear; bad training. Pal had wandered off as we talked and was digging and scratching here and there. I noticed that whenever Ruskin called to him or gave him a command, he responded nicely. His respect for Ruskin was strong, but would it be for me?

"I carry this pouch with me full of sweet stuff that Pal likes," Ruskin said. "After a good performance, I reward him."

"It sure looks all beat up and chewed!"

"Yeah, well, there have been times when Pal didn't want to wait. He wanted his reward before I was ready."

Pal had come over to me and was sniffing the cuffs of my pants.

"Remember, don't touch or pet him. He can't stand it."

What a shame, I thought. I would have loved to run my hand through that thick, soft fur, and I was sure that Pal would enjoy it. But lack of trust had made the bear so insecure that pleasures were forsaken in favor of fear.

"Okay, what do I do now?"

"It's pretty simple. Just go stand over there by that rock, then yell for Pal to come to you."

"That's all?"

"Yep, that's all. You might have to yell a few times, but he'll come."

I started for the rock. "Whatever you do," Ruskin shouted after me, "DON'T RUN!"

I stood in between two boulders, figuring that if I panicked, maybe I could run around behind the rocks (but knowing damn well that the bear could easily catch me). I took a deep breath, put my hands on my hips, and, in my most commanding voice, yelled, "Pal, come here!"

Pal stopped dead in his tracks and moaned. He held his head low to the ground with his ears back and fur bristled, but he stayed his ground.

"Pal! You heard me! Come here!"

He whipped around, raking the ground with his hind claws. Saliva was starting to drip from his jaws. I knew the next call would do it. My heart was beating a mile a minute. *What am I doing?* I thought. To invite a fully grown bear to come at you full tilt was scary, and ludicrous.

I yelled again, "Pal, get over here!"

That did it! With a rapid-fire chomping of his jaws and with his moan now turned into a banshee wail, Pal took off toward me, covering the ground with a sideways lope. Most people think that a bear stands up to attack. Not true. They come in low, grab for your legs or feet, knock you over, then maul and bite your prostrate body. My adrenaline was racing. A quick chill coursed through me. *What if Ruskin was wrong?* What if Pal had had a bad morning? If he did attack, what would I do? What hospital would I go to? I was doing all of this on blind faith—how stupid! I was young, and learning the hard way.

Pal was closing fast, and I felt he was so angry that he was really going to attack. He raced directly at me, kicking up dirt and dust. At the rate he was moving, there was no way he could stop in time. As he approached, I stiffened for the onslaught. At a distance of about five feet, he threw his head straight out toward my feet. With a high-pitched whine emanating from his throat, he pivoted his body around my feet at a fast speed. I felt his hot breath on my ankles. He literally shook the ground as his huge clawed feet raked three-inch grooves in the dirt, *very* close to my toes. My mind kept telling my body to respond—to move, to get away, to do something—but I held my position. Pal circled me time after time, roaring his anger. The ground was scarred in a complete circle. When the dust settled, Pal's anger slowly subsided, until finally he came to a standstill a few feet away.

I shot a look at Ruskin. He was in an alert position, tense but controlled. Pal started to sniff at my pant leg.

"Take off your belt and slip a loop around his neck," yelled Ruskin.

I reached down and carefully undid my belt buckle. Then, walking over to Pal, I gently lowered the belt and slipped it over his head. I could see his beady little eyes shifting back and forth from my hands and belt to my face. The belt was almost too small, and I could barely hold the tip.

"Bring him here," bellowed Ruskin.

I gently nudged Pal around and, partially bent over, I carefully edged my way to Ruskin with him.

"Well done, Ralph! You've got balls, that's for sure," Ruskin said, slipping the chain on Pal as I retrieved my belt. "Well, he's yours," he said. "Just send me 10 percent every time he works, until I get $500, and that's it."

✳

Although Pal respected me, he never really trusted anybody. Deep down he seemed to want to befriend me, but in the end he always backed away. Time and harsh training had hardened him. If I tried to touch him, his jaws would chomp, and he would race ahead a few feet to get away from my hand.

Pal's first job with me came when Walt Disney Studios needed a bear to run out of a bush, down a trail, and into the woods. The studio wanted to install a camera and three men in a hole on the trail, disguising the hole with tree limbs, branches, and ground cover. A large tree trunk would be placed in front of the camera so that when the bear came running down the trail he would jump *over* the camera, providing a terrific shot.

I arrived early in the morning to set up the shot. The scene was being shot on Disney's back lot. As a safety factor, workmen had constructed an eight-foot fence around the shooting area. I had withheld Pal's feed the night before so that he'd be sure to work for his reward. (Bears store up so much fat in their bodies that they can actually go a lot longer than one day without food, if necessary.) Pal's cage was moved with a forklift and deposited at the front of the trail. Bushes were placed to camouflage the cage, and an opening was left for Pal's emergence. A hole was then dug a hundred feet down the trail. A huge camera, a camera-man, and two assistants somehow fit into it, and the opening was covered up.

I stationed myself down the trail beyond the hole, with a pouch full of carrots, apples, candy bars, cookies, and a dozen other of Pal's favorites. Then, signaling the director that I was ready, I prepared to entice Pal to run down the trail to me, thus leaping over the hole.

At the director's call of "Action," my assistant raised the cage door, and Pal ambled out. I had a clicker in my hand to tell Pal where I was and to let him know that I had food for him. He smelled the food and headed toward me at the incredible speed of one mile per hour. You have never seen such a slow bear. The director yelled "Cut," we put the bear away, and we then listened to the director give us an ultimatum.

"The bear had better run," he said, "or I will see to it that you never work in this studio again!"

After an embarrassing second attempt, I ran to a phone. "Ruskin, this is Ralph. Yeah, listen, I need your help. How do I get Pal to run? Uh-huh, uh-huh, okay, yeah. Gotcha. Thanks a lot. I hope it works!"

I raced back to the set. The director hadn't come back yet. I asked the assistant director if we could have a car parked behind Pal's cage, with a row of bushes between them so Pal wouldn't see the car. I also asked that the car be rolled rather than driven into position.

Half an hour later, the director showed up. He gave me the evil eye. "Well, boy, is he going to do it?"

"Yes, sir," I said, hoping that Ruskin was a religious man who wouldn't lie.

This time, when the director yelled "Action," I cued my assistant to open the cage and at the same time to push a button, which flashed a red light behind the bush near the car. Upon seeing the light, the person in the car started it up and raced the engine. Well, you would have thought King Kong had just separated the bushes behind the car. Pal took off like a jet, his hind feet reaching forward to sink his claws into the earth, pushing off and propelling him through the air at maximum speed. Down the trail he came. Old Ruskin was right; for whatever reason, Pal was scared to death of motors.

I shot a look at the director. He was beaming. Pal was nearing the log, his great moment at hand. He jumped up on the log with sure speed, as though he would vault clear over the hole, but instead he stopped. He had smelled the men in the hole, and without hesitation he started to dig them up. He was going whole hog. Boards, branches, leaves, and twigs were flying in every direction. The men inside were screaming their heads off, running around in the hole like three blind mice as they tried to climb over one another to get out.

Pal took one last look at them and plunged right into the middle of the camera equipment and the three shrieking men—who then popped out of that hole as though they'd been shot from cannons.

In the midst of it all, I was trying to put a chain on Pal's neck. But he wasn't responding to any of my commands. Although he didn't attack, he threw me aside like a paper doll. Meanwhile, people were running in every direction. The only door in the arena was blocked behind the car, and no one wanted to risk passing the bear. Most people couldn't climb the fence; they were able to get up only a few feet. Pal was running around pulling all the people off the fence. Other times he would chase people and "snowball" right into them. Never have so many people run so fast.

Why Pal didn't bite anyone, no one knows—he certainly had the opportunity. It seemed that he was instead just punishing everyone for the ruse that had set him running. In any case, afterward old Pal just sat in the middle of all the goodies from the pouch, filling himself with junk food, burping and hiccuping. It wasn't until nightfall that I could get close enough to him to put a chain around his neck and take him home.

It took many months to convince Disney Studios that the occurrence had been, to say the least, unique. Plus, nobody had really gotten hurt. There were a few scraped knees, some torn pants, and a lot of hurt pride, but the incident taught me never to force or frighten a bear into doing anything he just doesn't want to do.

For many years, Pal provided the movie and TV industry with acting performances that thrilled and delighted animal lovers everywhere. For every animal performer there is always one job that stands above all others, and in Pal's case it went something like this: The studio was spending an exorbitant amount of money on a film called *Ice Palace,* starring Richard Burton and Robert Ryan. A sound stage had been built to match the Arctic, with glaciers, ice, and snow. Wind machines whipped the snow around the phoney (but believable) hills, forming drifts. For all intents and purposes, we were *in* the frozen Arctic.

The script called for a pregnant woman and her husband to be lost in a snow valley just as the baby is about to be born. The husband shoots a caribou and guts it, putting his wife inside the caribou's belly to keep warm. While the man is away, a bear comes along, apparently attracted by the blood. When he sees the mother and child, he rises up on his hind legs and attacks them. The returning husband sees the bear just in the nick of time and attacks him with his only weapon, a rather small knife.

I had stuck my neck out and told the studio that I could do the bear job—"No problem!" I figured at the time that *somewhere* there was a good, safe bear for wrestling. In those days, I was even willing to lose money on a job just to work at a major studio. It was the only way to get known, and the competition was tremendous.

I set to work. I figured I had one month to come up with the bear. Calls were made, places were visited, bears were seen. No one knew of a bear that could be wrestled safely. Even my competition had turned the job down because there weren't any good working bears around. I felt stupid. My ambition could mean my downfall. To promise something I couldn't provide would give me a bad reputation and seriously jeopardize any future jobs.

I called as far away as Canada but nowhere was there a bear that could be wrestled. One man had a Himalayan bear, but although it weighed maybe 300 pounds, it was only four feet tall. I'd look silly wrestling a bear on my knees. No, I needed a Northern black bear or a European brown bear that weighed 500 pounds or more and stood six or seven feet tall.

Of course, I did have Pal. In weight and size he was perfect for the job. I had trained him to walk upright and, towering above my head, he could walk thirty or forty feet. But he had never been touched. How could I wrestle a bear who wouldn't even let me pet him? I checked out a few bear suits, figuring I could have Pal walk in and then have the camera cut to another scene before cutting back to me, wrestling a man in a bear suit. God, how far could I sink! No, I'd gotten myself into this, and now I had to figure a way out.

One morning, I started to plan how to work with Pal. How could I show Pal that touching was okay, that I meant him no harm? I had an idea. Jumping into the car, I took off for Ellis Mercantile. A huge building in Hollywood, it survived as the largest establishment carrying props for use on the silver screen. Here you could find anything you could think of, from any period of time from the fifteenth century on.

I walked into the medieval section and found my answer: a suit of armor worn by a knight of the Round Table. In the film, the actor attacked by the bear is wearing a beautiful Eskimo parka.

My logic was to wear the armor under the parka to protect me from what I felt would be inevitable injury. King Arthur would have been proud. Loading the armor into the car, I took off for the ranch, eager to try it out.

Doug, my animal keeper, was the only person around. I alerted him to stay nearby in case I needed help. Gathering all the pieces together, I stood before a full-length mirror and slowly donned my metal garb. Pieces of mail, elbow joints, leg bands, chest plates—one by one, I hinged, tied, bolted, and pieced the suit together. Finally came the helmet. I had to remove my glasses to wear the helmet, which meant that I could then only see about eight feet around me; everything else was a blur.

Sir Galahad stared back at me from the mirror. With the music from *Camelot* in my ears, I clomped out into the sun to do battle.

Earlier, I had put Pal in a large outdoor working arena so he could run free, unhampered by a chain. My plan was to walk over and attempt to gently pet him. I felt that once he realized that petting felt good and that I wasn't going to hurt him, he would allow me to touch the rest of his body. Eventually, I figured, I should be able to wrestle around with him at least enough to get the shot; if he did bite me, the metal would protect me.

I opened the door to the arena and stood still for a moment, I could swear I heard trumpets blasting and people in the stands cheering. I must have looked like a moving junkyard as I slowly advanced to a black lump that I believed to be Pal. He had gone over to a small rise in the center of the ring and was awaiting my arrival.

As I noisily approached, I could see parts of Pal's body through the tiny slits in the helmet: first one of his legs, then his back, then his head. He was moving around, smelling and checking out this antique. I reached up and opened the faceplate so I could see him better. He had settled down and looked comfortable, as though awaiting a command.

I took a deep breath. The music stopped. The crowd was silent. With my metal hand, I gently touched his back. He leaped about four feet in a single bound, settling nearby. I turned and advanced, with gauntlet raised. Again, I reached to touch him. He moaned his dislike and moved further away. He came into focus as I headed in his direction. As I stretched my hand out to stroke him, my faceplate fell down. I stepped foward, reaching out, and as I did so, I believe I stepped on his foot.

The next thing I knew, there was a shearing pain in my arm, and I was aloft in the air, seemingly floating, until I crashed onto the ground about ten feet away. Pal had apparently swiped my feet out from under me after crunching my arm with his mouth.

As I hit the ground, I realized—too late—that Pal's jaws would bend the metal into my flesh, and that the metal wouldn't flex back. I was face down in the dirt, trying to turn over, when I felt a heavy weight land on my back and stay there. I felt my leg being picked up and dropped with a crash . . . then my arm. I heard a crunch each time. Pal was biting the metal. All of a sudden, I was being thrown and pulled and pushed around. Again he landed on top of me, and I realized what he was doing: he was trying to open the suit like a can opener. He wanted to get inside. I felt as though the crowd had given me the thumbs-down treatment, and that the victor—Pal, in this case—was giving me the *coup de grace.* It was hot and sweaty in the suit, and the dust blowing in through the mask was turning into mud. I was a mess.

Where do I come up with these ideas? Whose side of my family can I blame it on? Voices yelling and screaming brought me back to my senses. I felt the arena guard drag my limp form across the ground. My faceplate was removed, and I looked up into the faces of Laura, the stuntwoman, my wife Toni, and one of the keepers. Apparently, they had just been driving in when the keeper ran over to inform them of my predicament.

It took saws, hammers, screwdrivers, and a vise to free me from my metal prison. The cuts and bruises were many, but the worst injury was to my pride. As the week of healing wore on, I realized that my chances of coming up with another bear were not likely. I couldn't let the studio down. I was committed. I decided to wrestle Pal!

I set my plan. I would station the best men available close to the action. A few fire extinguishers would be nearby, to be used to scare Pal away, if necessary. The parka was bulky enough for

101

some heavy padding to be slipped underneath. I would get Pal to walk upright into the camera, and at the last second I'd launch myself from a snow embankment just in front of the camera, hitting him high and fast. The director had told me that he needed only a short piece of film, so the hit and a quick roll would do it. I figured Pal would attack me in the arm or hand, and maybe in the side by my rib cage. I knew my men would get him off me after the first attack, and an ambulance would rush me off for medical care. I put my plan in order, then sat back waiting for the critical day to come.

I arrived on the set early in the morning with Pal in tow and four of my best trainers to assist me. As usual, we had withheld Pal's feed the night before. The set was large and chilly, or maybe it just appeared to be cold, with icicles, snowdrifts, and snow-laced trees everywhere. It was a complete Arctic landscape, even rounded off with a cold blue sky. An ambulance parked nearby reminded me of the pain I was about to endure.

I brought Pal around to the back of the artificial forest and tied him to a tree. I then stationed the trainers in the positions that best suited me for an emergency. They all knew what was about to happen and thought I was crazy. However, no finer men existed, and I knew that when the chips were down, I could count on them.

The camera was set, and instructions were given. Wardrobe dressed me in the appropriate garb, and I inserted pads and protective clothing wherever I could. Then, taking a deep breath, I stepped out. I was as ready as I was ever going to be.

The prop man handed me a fake knife. I pulled the hood of my parka over my head, thinking this would make good protection for my neck and face. Except for my brief armored experience with him in the arena, this was to be the first—and probably the last—time that Pal would be touched.

The lights were throwing a bluish glow across the "frozen wasteland" as I took my position to the right of the camera, three feet up on a snow embankment. With knife in hand, I alerted my men to take Pal out and stand by, and then I nodded that I was ready. *Ready?* I thought to myself. Ready to be bitten? Where?

How much pain? Will I be disfigured? I heard the director yell, "Action!"

This was it!

I called Pal and gave him his "Up!" command. Like a true star, he came out of the sparse forest standing fully upright. He looked immense. I crouched for the spring: fifteen feet . . . ten feet . . . five feet . . . NOW! I leaped. I landed straight on Pal's chest, catching him off guard. With one hand I grabbed for a tuft of hair to hang onto, and with the other I stabbed him with the fake knife.

The next thing I remember is his two gigantic forearms bearing down on me. Pal's viselike grip held me to him like a babe to its mother. Wet snow brushed against my cheek. We were down, rolling over and over on the slope. In those moments, which seemed to last a lifetime, I saw beady, sparkling eyes, six-inch claws, shiny white fangs, and lots of long black hair.

When the director yelled "Cut," I realized I was alone. Pal had wandered off, and I knew the boys would guide him into his cage. I heard people rushing up to me, their shoes crunching in the snow. Time had slowed down for me since I'd jumped into Pal's arms. Everything had been so vivid that I'd seen the tiniest details, but that sense was now fading fast. It was as though I was awakening from a dream. My eyes opened, and I saw people, boots, snow. Hands grabbed me.

"Are you okay, Ralph?" asked four people at once.

"I think so," I said. It was impossible! I checked myself all over—not a scratch, not a drop of blood.

"Great fight!" complimented the director.

The pats on the back, the handshakes, and the congratulations all faded away as I walked over to Pal's cage. He was lying down, head on his paws, gazing off into space. I sat down beside him and looked into his eyes. Why, Pal? Why didn't you hurt me? I wondered to myself. Perhaps we had finally gained some mutual understanding for one another.

Pal lifted his head and licked my hand.

11

ELEPHANTS NEVER FORGET

"Get up, there!" A sixteen-foot cattle whip snapped the air. The crack was sharp and absolute. "Elmer, move on out! Emma, get in line!"

A train of twenty-three wagons, each pulled by horses, strained up a grassy, forty-five-degree hill. Forty or fifty men, women, and children walked beside them, some carrying goods, others leading goats and sheep. In between the wagons were six full-sized camels.

Further down the wagon train, four zebras moved along, bridled and with their lead ropes tied to the back of the wagons, horse-style. Various monkeys, dogs, and pigs ran to and fro.

Printed in big, colorful letters across the canvas side of the lead wagon were the words "FRONTIER CIRCUS." And that's what it was—a traveling circus on wheels, typical of the late nineteenth and early twentieth centuries. Even though this was the 1970s, it took an onlooker only a moment to feel as though he were back in the days when Wyatt Earp and Billy the Kid roamed the West.

A show like this would travel from town to town and in each stop would set up overnight a full one-ring circus, complete with trapeze artists, a fat woman, a thin man, midgets, juggling acts, and a wild-animal menagerie, complete with a special lion or tiger act.

This was the television series "Frontier Circus," which starred Chill Wills and John Derek and featured a special guest star every week. I had acquired the contract to supply all the exotic animals for the series. It was one of our biggest jobs, and we were going all-out to make it the best. Every day, dozens of our wild animals performed their roles on camera, and some were the stars of the show.

Things were going along great until one morning when I received an early telephone call from the director.

"Ralph, this is J. B. Listen, I know we just wrapped the last show of the season, but I wanted to tell you what was coming up in a few months."

"Yeah."

"At the start of next season's series we'll need an elephant!" He said it as though an elephant was an item I carried around in my back pocket. "You have *got* one, haven't you?" he asked, following a slight hesitation on my part. "Haven't you?" he asked again.

"Sure, of course," I said, with my fingers crossed. "I was just writing it down. When do you need it?"

"About September. Three months should give you enough time to teach it its act."

"Act?" I asked.

"Yeah, you know—sitting up, bowing, hopping, all that kind of stuff."

"Uh . . . sure, no problem," I said. "Just send me the script so we can get started practicing."

I hung up, after assuring J. B. that we would have the best elephant act this side of the Ringling Brothers.

"Who was that?" asked Toni.

"Studio," I said.

"Oh! What did they want?"

"An elephant."

"Hmmm. Where are you going to get one?"

"I don't know."

"Hmmm. Did you tell them you had one?"

"Yeah."

"Why did you do that?"

" 'Cause I was afraid of losing the contract."

"Well," she said facetiously, "you can always hang a rubber hose from the milk cow's head. That should do it."

"Funny, Toni! Very funny."

For the next five days, we called everybody we knew to see if anyone had heard of an elephant for sale. A few turned up, priced at around $10,000 each—way over our budget. Plus, one of them was a "batter"—that is, an elephant that throws its trunk at you with the intent to do bodily harm. We even had a couple of offers from zoos, but none of their elephants were tame, let alone trained.

By the end of the week, things were looking pretty grim. I knew my competition had an elephant, and that if they got wind of the job they could take over the series.

"Even if we did find one," said Toni, "for—how much did you say?"

"A thousand dollars," I replied.

"—a thousand dollars," she continued, "what would you haul it in?"

"I don't know. Maybe its owner would bring it."

We had exhausted just about every means of finding an elephant when a friend showed me a newspaper ad. It read: "For Sale: old female circus elephant with bad eye, to professional people only. Cheap." It gave a phone number for somewhere back East—we weren't sure where. I called.

"Hello?" a rather burly-sounding voice bellowed in my ear. I could hear kids screaming in the background.

"I read your ad in the Sunday paper about an elephant for sale. Is she still available?"

"Yeah, we got her. She ain't much to look at, and she needs some meat an' potatoes, if you know what I mean," he belched out.

"How much do you want for her?"

"A thousand dollars, mister—that's it. She's a steal. Not many around at that price."

"What's wrong with her? I mean, any defects, bad habits?" I figured that for that price there had to be something wrong.

"Look—take her or leave her. If you want her, fine. If not, well, we'll just cook her up and feed her to the dogs. Ha!"

There had been a beat before his answer that told me to believe nothing. I could just visualize this guy—baldheaded, overweight, shirtless, and unshaven.

"Look, I gotta go," he said.

"Okay," I said. "I'll take her."

"You will?" came his surprised answer.

"Yeah. But we're coming all the way from California. It'll take about a week to get there. Will you hold her for us?"

"If I don't get too tired, holding all that weight! Ha!"

What a jerk, I thought.

"Send me a few bucks so I know you're for real, and you've got yourself an elephant," he said.

We exchanged telephone numbers and addresses. As I was hanging up, I asked, "Oh, by the way, what's her name?"

" 'Modoc'—at least, that's the name she came with. But the locals here call her 'One-Eye Mo'."

We picked up a used van-trailer for about $500. The sides were rusted and some of the tires were bald, but with some oil, a lube job, and some new tires, she looked pretty roadworthy. As for the truck, an old Chevy "bobtail" that had been impounded for nonpayment was being auctioned off at the police garage—and we hit it lucky.

Everybody we knew pitched in to fix up the trailer. We laid in a new, two-inch plywood floor to support Modoc's weight. Holes were drilled in the plywood, and heavy leg chains were run through. We then installed lightweight panel boards around the inside to prevent any "nosing" around with the electric cables running through the trailer to the sidelights and the back brake lights.

All the while, everyone was telling us we were crazy to embark on such a risky venture—after all, we were spending all the money we'd just earned from the series, money that was badly needed for the ranch facilities for cage repairs, old bills, and the like. True, the deal *did* sound pretty scary. I had never heard of an elephant selling for $1,000! Either she was on her last legs, or she was a killer rejected by the circus . . . or both. And if the elephant didn't work out, what use would we have for the truck and the trailer?

But, if we were lucky enough to be able to use her even a little bit, then the new contract was ours—and there would be enough money to do all the rest.

✹

Frank, my ranch foreman, and I took off one early morning, heading for the small town in Vermont where Modoc was then residing. Neither one of us had ever driven a twenty-two-wheel truck and trailer before, but after a thousand miles or so each, we'd stopped grinding gears. Except for an occasional flat tire on our "new" retreads, the four-day trip went smoothly.

Seeing the country from high up in the cab was a new experience. The size and weight of our rig gave us a feeling of power and great energy as we sped across the deserts of Arizona and lugged up the Rocky Mountains. Texas seemed to take forever, but the Plains states flew by—and from Chicago on, we were on the edge of our seats anticipating our arrival.

I had never owned an elephant before, but I was experienced in handling them for others. Always one of my favorites in the world of animals, elephants never failed to leave me in awe. I found them to be both extremely intelligent and very sensitive.

I remember in particular a photographic safari I took to East Africa. It had been raining for days, and the earth had turned into three feet of mud. A mother rhino and her baby had ventured across an open area in search of some salt that a rancher had put out for the animals. They finally found a rather large amount of salt, and they spent the next twenty minutes slurping it up. The mother then moved away, heading toward the forest. The baby attempted to follow, but found itself stuck fast in the mud. It howled to get free. The mother returned, sniffed, walked around her baby, and then headed toward the forest once more. Again the baby called to her. This went on for some time. Meanwhile, the rain had started to beat down, and the struggling baby was losing its strength. The mother rhino just didn't have the intelligence to help it.

Out of the forest came a group of elephants, heading for the salt lick. The mother rhino, sensing danger, charged the lead elephant, who quickly sidestepped the assault. The elephants were content to find another salt lick about a hundred feet from the baby. The mother rhino, feeling that all was safe, left the baby to forage in the nearby woods.

One adult male elephant with a fairly large set of tusks left the salt lick and approached the baby rhino. He touched the baby with the tip of his trunk, checking out its heavy body and buttocks. I was amazed at what happened next! The elephant got down on his knees, placed his tusks deep down under the baby, and began to lift.

Just then, out of the forest came mama, at a dead run. She charged the elephant, who gracefully sidestepped her and headed back to his salt lick.

This pattern continued for the next few hours. The elephant would attempt to help, and the mother would charge, thinking her baby was being threatened. Finally, the herd of elephants moved on.

The baby rhino, exhausted from the struggle and suffering from exposure, just lay there, too tired to move. By morning the mother had moved off to feed elsewhere.

A game warden and I had planned to sneak over quickly and help the baby before its mother came back. As we approached, the baby began to struggle and bawl loudly. Knowing the mother would be on her way, we took off fast. We looked back just in time to see the baby break free. The mother returned, and both she and baby then ambled off into the thicket.

While the primitive nature of the rhino mother had prevented her from using her horn to get her baby out of the mud, the elephant *knew* that the baby was in trouble and needed help, and he saw exactly how to administer that help. I was thrilled to have had the opportunity to witness such a feat. Over the years I would witness many other feats of elephant courage, ingenuity, and helpfulness—though what lay ahead for the particular elephant I was en route to was yet unknown.

✸

Pulling off the main highway, we entered a small community. After some searching, we finally managed to find the old, dilapidated, one-story house. A broken porch and a yard full of tin cans and old tires gave it a look of depression.

We knocked on the door. It seemed that nobody was home, but the door was cracked open a bit. I could see that the inside of the house was in about the same condition as the outside.

"Hello! Anybody here?"

No answer. Walking around the side of the house and across the yard, we noticed a couple of boys pitching rocks at what appeared to be a large tree. We were heading toward the boys when the voice I'd heard on the telephone boomed out: "Hey, you! You're on private property!"

There was the man, almost identical to how I had visualized him—fat, balding, and gruff.

"We're the people who called you from California—came to get Modoc," I said.

"Well, you really *did* come, after all," he said, ambling over to us. "Thought you might forfeit the money." He wiped his dirty hands on his dirty trousers.

"I'm Ralph, and this is Frank."

"Bo Jenkins."

We shook hands all around. I could smell that familiar circus odor drifting through the air, but I couldn't figure out where it was coming from. Then I heard a squeal that sounded as though it had come from a hurt animal.

"I got 'er!" yelled one of the kids.

"You kids go on home now."

"I got 'er, Mr. Jenkins! Square in the leg! Here's your money." I saw the kids give Jenkins a couple of coins. "I don't have to pay for the second one, right?"

"Yeah, sure, kid. Go on, now—beat it!" he said. An embarrassed smirk crossed his reddening face. He quickly changed the subject. "Come on, I'll show you Mo."

We walked over to a four-foot-high barbed-wire fence encircling a lot of roughly two acres. It was barren except for a few shrubs, dozens of beer cans and soda-pop bottles, and an unusually large number of stones at the far end of the field. There, a large dead oak tree straddled the fence. Tied to the base of the tree was a heavy tow chain. It stretched out about fifteen feet and was shackled to the foot of an enormous elephant.

This was Modoc. She was the tallest Indian elephant I had ever seen. She looked to be around thirty to forty years old. A bent tin sign hung on a pole just out of her reach. It read "One-Eye Mo—Killer Elephant. KEEP YOUR DISTANCE!" The sign was full of rock holes and dents.

I felt my face flush with anger. "What do you do? Have the local kids pay you so they can throw rocks at the elephant?"

"Naw! Well, just a few. It helps pay the food bill."

By the looks of this elephant, she hadn't seen a proper meal or even eaten in a long, long time.

"Look here, mister," demanded Jenkins, "you either take her or forfeit your deposit. I just don't care one way or the other."

Frank was fuming. "Good Lord, Ralph, we can't show her on camera! The Humane Society people would hang us!"

"I know," I said, "but we can't leave her here in this condition." I turned to Jenkins. "What does that sign mean, 'Killer'? Is she dangerous?"

"I don't know," he replied. "I was told she is, but I never gave her a chance to show me."

"You mean you never approach her? Clean or scrub or treat her for worms?!"

"*Her?!* No way! Hell, no! What do you think I am, crazy? You want to get me killed?!"

Frank and I were ready to deck him. "How long have you had her?" I asked.

"Twenty years."

"*Twenty years!!* You mean she's been here like this for twenty years?!" I must have had a look of murder on my face, because Jenkins started to back away.

"Look, if you want her, fine, I'll be in the house. If not—see ya." He turned and headed toward the house at a rather fast pace.

We both took a deep breath and, holding the barbed wire for each other, climbed through the fence and headed for Mo. As we approached, we saw that she was resting her head against the old tree. She had apparently been doing this for some time, since a

ultan, a cross-breed of Siberian and Bengal species, poses with me for a portrait. Although I gen-
rally disapprove of interbreeding tigers, some have come to me with various subspecies already
red into them. Sultan exhibited the best qualities of the two species: the larger size of the Siberian
nd the more pliant intelligence of the Bengal.

Clarence the cross-eyed lion, one of the stars of the TV series "Daktari." Although we initially tried to correct Clarence's eye condition, we learned that it did not impair his vision, and so we left it as nature had intended.

Putting one's arm into the jaws of a lion can be a terrible mistake unless the lion knows not to apply too much pressure. Here I am teaching Zamba how much pressure he can exert by tugging firmly on his whiskers.

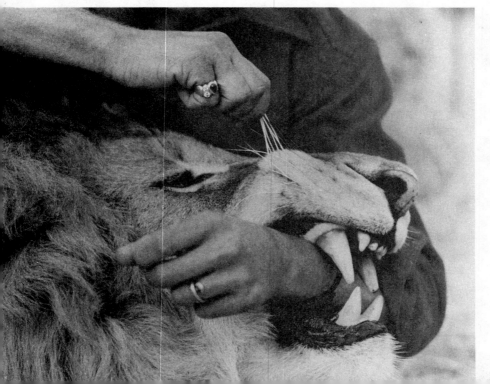

Joy Adamson, author of *Born Free*, met Tammy while on a fundraising visit to the United States. My partner, Ivan Tors (far right), and I were happy to see that Tammy made Ms. Adamson feel at home.

William Holden was a true conservationist as well as a good friend. His understanding of African wildlife reached a new high during the filming of *The Lion*. Here he takes a break while Tammy asks for attention.

To my recollection, Twiga was the only giraffe in the United States that had been trained to allow a human to ride him. Twiga was 8 years old, 15 feet tall, and still growing at the time of this photo. The saddle was 1½ feet tall in front but only 2½ *inches* high in the rear to compensate for the giraffe's sharply slanted back.

On cue, Sultan hits me at 30 miles an hour during a training session. I relaxed my body to take the blow, but he still hurled me 10 feet before I came crashing back to earth, whereupon he scooped me up in his paws as you or I might scoop up a pet rabbit. Throughout the exercise he kept his claws sheathed and his fangs unexposed. Affection training worked!

My daughter, Tana, reads a bedtime story to Zamba. Both were raised on affection training, and each developed a sincere love for the other.

Amanda Blake and Mickey Rooney were cohosts of the PATSY ceremonies when I received an award from the American Humane Society for outstanding achievement in motion pictures.

We posed with Loch Ness, a 200-pound, 26-foot African rock python, after he had destroyed an apartment at the Mount Kenya Safari Club by turning on the faucets and flooding the place. From left to right are a field trainer, Capucine, Pamela Franklin, William Holden, Trevor Howard, Stuart Raffel, and me.

Gentle Ben relaxes his 600 pounds on my shoulders during a morning workout on the set of his popular TV series.

Sonny and Cher pose with Modoc, Toni, and me during production of their first film, *Good Times,* which was shot at our ranch in 1967.

My wife, Toni, and I share two black leopard cubs with John Wayne. The cubs were born on St. Croix during the filming of *The Island of Dr. Moreau*.

Toni and I take a break with Burt Lancaster during filming of *The Island of Dr. Moreau*. Sixty-five lions, tigers, leopards, and other exotic animals were used in the production.

My "family" of chimpanzees gather around to watch as trainers bring two Bengal tigers onto the set of "Daktari." I think the chimps all hoped they would not do a scene with the tigers that day.

C. J. the orangutan gives me a hug before shooting a scene with Bo Derek for the film *Tarzan the Apeman*. Tell me there's no resemblance!

Many nights I would find this duckling curled up in one of C. J.'s massive, hairy arms. The powerful orangutan would gently stroke the duckling's head with one of his large fingers — a rare and touching sight to behold.

Tana rides the two-ton hippo Nayla in this extremely rare photo. Hippos are considered dangerous animals, but we succeeded in winning over Nayla, the only affection-trained hippo in the world.

Tana, Toni, and me in a family portrait with Clarence. Tana often referred to Clarence as her "big brother."

In the annals of the motion picture and TV industries, no child has ever worked in complete safety with an African lion until Pamela Franklin teamed up with Zamba for *The Lion*. Their affection for each other continued long after filming was finished.

Here I am with (left to right) Debbie, Taj, Modoc, and Misty — each a great performer in his or her own right.

Margie the elephant was one of Tana's favorite "living" toys. Margie would sometimes pick up Tana with her trunk and put her on her back, where Tana would take her afternoon siesta. If Tana started to slide off, Margie would extend her trunk and adjust the child's position.

After being abused for 20 years by a previous owner who promoted him as a "killer elephant," Modoc, one of the largest elephants in captivity, is welcomed by Tana and Toni to the ranch, his new home.

I am sitting astride the two-ton rhinoceros Matadi. Matadi had been well taught through affection training, but the rhinoceros shown in the background had not. As soon as this photo was taken, that rhino charged at me. I dismounted and interposed Matadi between myself and the massive animal — a kind of ring around the rhino!

large worn spot grazed the tree at the same height as her head. She slowly turned toward us, her great ragged ears slowly angling forward, capturing every sound we made.

As we got closer, we could see just how abused she was. She was about a thousand pounds underweight. Her huge backbone arched high in the air, and her skin was stretched taut across a skeletal rib cage, only to hang loosely in huge globs at the bottom of her stomach. She appeared to be blind in her left eye.

It was then that I saw it—from afar, one would never notice, since it was on the far side of the tree—*the end of the heavy tow chain disappeared into her ankle.* The chain had been there so long without being removed that the outer skin had actually grown over it. It left the leg looking as though it had an overlarge ankle.

"My God! Frank! That bastard! That dirty bastard!" I turned, heading back toward the house.

Frank stopped me. "Time for that later," he said.

We stood there, amazed at the total emaciation of the poor old girl. There were bruises and cuts by the dozens, obviously made by the stone-throwing. Old, healed gouges showed where large rocks had taken their toll. The hair was missing from Mo's tail, and I recalled having seen an elephant-hair bracelet on Jenkins's wrist. I wondered to myself how he had managed that!

I called to her: "Hi, Mo. . . . Hi, old girl. . . ." She raised her great head high in the air, and for a moment she was silent. Then she made a "whooshh" sound with her trunk and stepped forward toward us. I could hear a distinct grumbling deep down in her stomach. She seemed to beg for us to come to her. I could see her bad eye. It wasn't so bad to look at, actually—there was just a white cast where the pupil should have been.

Modoc started to come to life. She was swaying and anxious.

"What do we do, Ralph?" Frank asked. "She hasn't been off those chains in twenty years!"

Both Frank and I were carrying what is called a "bull hook" in the business. It consists of a hardwood handle, which can vary in length from one to three feet and which has an iron core (or chrome, on the more expensive types); a hook attached at the end and angled gently to one side; and a point that juts straight out.

The hook part is used for pulling elephants around or bringing the head down or the foot up. The probe is for moving them to one side, forward, or backward. The sharpness of the point is critical: you should be able to hang it from your index finger without drawing blood. Some fear trainers sharpen the point for harsher treatment. We have never found that necessary. In fact, it's downright dangerous to do so, as it can cause a great deal of pain, instilling a "survival mode" in the elephant (the animal may develop an attitude problem toward the trainer). Properly used, it is merely a small guide—ideally, simply an extension of one's hand—against the immensity of the elephant.

We approached Mo straight on, talking gently. She was straining against her chain so hard that it was ripping out of her flesh. The open cracks oozed with blood and pus. Sometimes in our business, we must make decisions that could mean life or death to us, decisions based on one's ability to read the animal—in this case, a nine-foot-tall, maybe four-ton elephant with the potential to kill in an instant. My natural instincts were at work. I felt that these were not the actions of a dangerous animal, but rather of one that was affectionate and starved, an elephant that craved the touch of human hands.

I laid the hook down, and with outstretched hands I walked toward Mo. She leaned forward, stretching out her trunk. I reached over and gently touched its tip. It seemed that to her this was like receiving an electric shock, or, more accurately, a jolt of pure energy. At what I believe must have been her first human touch in many, many years, she started to trumpet. Tail held high, head up, ears forward, she pranced around. I was thrilled. What ecstasy!

I moved in close. Mo gently laid her trunk over my shoulder, ran it down the full length of my body and encircled the tip around my toe. Then she started to shake. Her belly rumbled. As a naturalist, I knew this was her way of greeting me. Yet, as an animal lover, I also knew this was the sobbing of joy, expressing years of pent-up pain and hunger and the deprivation of solitary confinement.

Many times I have witnessed strong displays of emotion from

animals that have become accustomed to the companionship of another animal or person and have then lost that pleasure, for whatever reason. Animals, like people, experience loneliness, boredom, and despondency when the comfort of a friendly voice, a familiar smell, or a gentle touch no longer brightens their day.

Frank went around by the tree and started to work on the chain. It took many trips to the truck for equipment to finally cut away the chain. We left a small extension of it leading to her ankle, as we knew that a veterinarian would need to be there when we took it off. We cut a hole in the fence, and slowly, for the first time in twenty years, Mo walked—quivering, and dragging her stiff, chained leg across her prison yard—to freedom.

When she saw the truck, she bellowed, as though it should answer back. Perhaps it reminded her of one of the circus vehicles of years past. Many people had gathered when they heard the bellowing. Adults hugged their children tightly as "Killer Mo" limped by. She walked up the ramp and into the truck. Frank had laid a nice carpet of straw for her to rest in and provided an ample pile of fresh alfalfa for her to eat. We put the end of a garden hose in her mouth and turned it on, and for five minutes she filled herself with gallons of fresh water.

Frank went to the house, paid the balance, and got a bill of sale. I knew that if I had gone, I would probably have punched Jenkins's lights out.

We didn't want Mo to back out the rear door while we were on the road or do any structural damage inside the trailer, so we tied one of her legs, for safety reasons. Patting the old girl's derriere, we closed the ten-foot door, revved up the engine, and slowly drove down the driveway. We had ourselves an elephant!

The states passed quickly, as did the days and nights. We stopped every few hours to check and see that Mo was riding comfortably and that her leg chain was secure. We kept the floor covered with fresh straw, and we fed Mo about a fourth of an elephant's normal daily intake (concerned that a normal-sized diet might be too rich), placing twenty to thirty pounds of alfalfa well within reach of her trunk. Four times a day, we gave her five gallons of a special mix of grains. Powdered penicillin from our first-aid kit was sprinkled in the leg wound morning, afternoon, and night, and the wound was kept as clean and sterile as possible to prevent infection.

The gas stations along the way were very helpful when we asked for a drink of water for our elephant. Modoc would pick up the hose with her trunk and place it in her mouth. When I saw her control the flow of water by stepping on the hose, I began to suspect that this lady had a history. On hot days she would suck water up in her trunk and spray her back to stay cool.

Other times, we would take her out for walks to keep her from getting stiff from standing in one place for too long, and to get good circulation going in her injured leg. During one of these walks, we caused a major jam-up on the highway—everybody wanted to see the elephant. Some cars even pulled off to the side so the children could see Mo up close.

In Texas, the temperature was approaching 101 degrees. When we asked a gas-station owner who had some property behind his station if we could use it to bathe the elephant, he happily agreed. We bought some laundry soap and a scrub brush from a local grocery store and set to work. We scrubbed and scrubbed, pouring the laundry soap and water over Mo until she looked like one giant bubble. She seemed to thoroughly enjoy the scrubbing, and occasionally she'd raise a foot and let out a squeaky sound when we found a ticklish spot on her ribs, just behind her left front leg. It must have been her first bath in years.

It took us a while to get through the crust and the scabs, but finally we laid her down and washed one side of her thoroughly. Her skin appeared a sleek, gray color. Her cheekbones and the bottoms of her ears had a pinkish cast, confirming my previous estimate of her age. I carefully flushed out her eyes, paying particular attention to the left one.

The sun dried her quickly, and her spirits seemed to be lifted. We tipped the gasoline attendant a ten, and walked Mo back to the truck. For all her previous wear and tear, she looked immaculate.

Two days later we reached New Mexico. We stopped at a telephone booth to call the ranch to let everyone know that we were on our way. My daughter Tana, eight, was ecstatic with the idea of befriending an elephant for the first time. Toni said that everyone was anxious to see us and our new family member. The studio had called to ask how the training was coming, and she had told them it was "rolling along" quite well.

By now, we had learned how to drive a truck and trailer with an elephant on board. Elephants tend to rock considerably to maintain good blood circulation. However, when you have four tons up off the ground, rocking back and forth, the handling of the trailer becomes difficult. There is a danger of turning over, especially if the elephant is rocking to the right, as you go around a right-hand turn. But by the time we hit Arizona, we were doing quite well. Every time we crossed a state border, the state police had us unload Mo, as her constant rocking prevented an accurate reading at the weigh station.

A day and a half later, we rolled into the ranch early in the morning. All the smells of the other animals must have brought back some memories that excited Modoc, for she let out trumpet after trumpet, blasting the air all the way up the half-mile entrance. We followed suit by blasting our diesel horn. Modoc was home!

The horses and zebras bolted and raced around their pens, and the macaws and peacocks shrieked. The camels looked on, munching, while the ostriches ran in zigzag patterns, looking like ballerinas in tutus. Everyone came out to greet Mo. We jumped out of the cab into the arms of our loved ones and the accolades of the group. Then we went around to the back door, put down the ramp, and walked in. We undid Mo's leg chain and slowly backed her out of the trailer. For the next few hours, she was lavished with care, and with goodies: popcorn (to make her feel at home), candy, soda pop, cookies, bread. She even ate a bouquet of flowers that had been brought for her arrival!

A reconstructed garage became her new house. A thin, light-weight, fifty-foot chain was attached to her good hind leg, giving her complete access to the outdoors as well as to the interior of the garage. She could have broken the chain at any time, but she never even tried. A large bathtub filled with water was at her constant disposal.

On that first day we stayed with Mo until nightfall. Then Toni gave her a kiss on the cheek and turned out the lights. After Tana had poured a few extra quarts of grain on the alfalfa pile and kissed the tip of Mo's trunk, we all left, feeling really good!

The vet arrived early the next morning. He took one look at Modoc's condition and told us that we'd gotten her out just in the nick of time. She would never have survived another winter back there.

We went to work on her nails, which were overgrown, gnarled, and broken. We worked for hours clipping, filing, and rasping, but I figured it would be months before they would be back to normal.

The vet then wormed her, treated her minor cuts and injuries, and put her on some fast-acting vitamins and mineral supplements. Checking her teeth, he found he had to "float" the back ones. Sometimes, due to a poor diet, an animal's back molars will grow sharp points that prevent the teeth from grinding food properly. "Floating" is done by rasping the points off with a large steel file, making the molars flat and more efficient.

Toni and Tana cleaned her ears, which caused her to emit a very high shriek, as it apparently tickled. Then we all concentrated on the big problem . . . her ankle. The vet felt that major surgery was needed, but in Mo's weakened condition, it was too risky to put her under an anesthetic. So he decided to use a local painkiller and depend on her good nature and mild attitude to allow him to work.

We brought Mo to a small, clean pad of cement, which was normally used for washing down the camels and hoofed stock. Giving her a command to "come down" and another to "come over," we laid her down and prepared her for surgery. Once the drugs had taken effect, the vet began to cut the hide along the top of the heavy chain with a large surgical knife, with the aim of cutting a complete circle. The cutting was so difficult that we had to take turns holding and separating the thick hide. The skin was exceptionally tough, and penetrating it was very hard work.

Once the vet had cut completely through, he gently used a small scalpel to part the flesh all the way to the embedded chain. Even though he had given Mo a blood coagulant, she was still bleeding profusely. Toni assisted by dabbing gauze and cotton swabs after each cut. Frank kept Mo lying quietly with gentle persuasion and touching.

That she hadn't died of infection or tetanus was amazing, the vet said. Her body had built up a tough wall of gristlelike flesh surrounding the chain. The rust from the chain had penetrated the area and turned it a dark brown. We cut the main bolt holding the chain around the leg. I took one end and the vet took the other, and together we slowly lifted it away from the raw flesh, uprooting its twenty-year implant. In places it was held fast by the skin growth, but a quick cut with the scalpel set it free. Once it was out, we went to work washing and disinfecting the trench, which was about two inches deep. The bleeding continued, so Mo was given more coagulants.

Suturing was impossible. The excessive, or "proud," flesh was trimmed off to promote growth, shots were given, bandages applied, and a specially constructed shield cast was strapped into place over the wound. It was shaped like a cone and served to protect against dirt and Modoc's probing trunk. Her good eye was searching back and forth, trying to see what was going on. On Frank's command of "up," Modoc threw her legs out and up. Then, bringing them down hard, she pulled herself up into a sitting position, and finally she stood up.

Mo was kept dry and warm, and her bandages were changed daily. Painkillers were injected as often as we felt she needed them. For the next few weeks she favored the other foot, keeping the pressure off the injured one.

The weeks passed, and Mo's overall condition continually improved. Although she had a long way to go, the wrinkles in her skin had begun to disappear, as she had gained a couple of hundred pounds. The new television season's shooting was coming near, and after consultation with the vet, it was decided that a few short and easy training sessions would be acceptable.

We had built some sturdy pedestals and set them up inside a circular area the size of a circus arena. Around it we had placed cut oak logs, to serve as the perimeter. Quite a few of the staff had gathered to watch Modoc go through her paces. We moved one of the oak logs so that she could enter the arena. As I was stooped down replacing it, I heard a gasp from the onlookers. I stood up and turned around to one of the most phenomenal sights I have ever witnessed.

Modoc had walked to the center of the ring while I was putting the log back in place. Someone had found some old circus music and had turned it on, and the music of the calliope sounded across the arena. Suddenly, she had started to dance. When I turned, there she was, performing on her own in the dusty, old arena. Her massive frame shook and quivered.

I couldn't believe it. What she was doing was impossible. I mean, *no* animal performs without a trainer—at least, I'd never seen it done. Plus, whatever the reason, she hadn't performed in twenty years! How was this possible? Here she was, dancing like a seasoned performer, pirouetting and swirling, doing hops and skips, waltzes, leg-ups, and pedestal work. She was circling the arena—one, two, three, waltz; one, two, three, waltz. Her muscles were weak from years of inactivity, and her sore foot must have made it difficult, but she was doing it! Trunk up, head held high, Modoc wasn't in this old arena—she was in a circus tent, on a sawdust floor, swirling to the music beneath a spotlight. She was a star of the big top, with thousands of people applauding. There were clowns and children, and cotton candy—"Step right up! See the big show!" It was all there. The memories, the smells, the laughter, the applause. Modoc ended her act with a bow, and the music stopped. The huge audience dwindled to those few who were standing on the fence or seated on the top rail.

We were all speechless, teary-eyed at what we had just seen. Modoc stood, waiting quietly. It was then that I looked down and saw the blood oozing from her ankle. She had opened the wound.

Then came the applause, the whistles, the congratulations. We all rushed to her with hugs and kisses and many "well done" pats, and then we gently headed her back to the barn for treatment. True, her performance had been somewhat shaky and uneven, and some of it she hadn't been able to do at all. But she had *tried!*

I knew then that this lady must have been a star—a great star—to be able to perform in the ring without a trainer. She must have been world renowned.

Modoc rose to stardom again. This time it was in films and on television, in such productions as *The Greatest Show on Earth*, *Clarence the Cross-Eyed Lion*, and "Daktari."

PART IV

GIMMICKS
AND GADGETS

Purple ducks, brontosauruses with fins, tigers with horns, talking orangutans—anything is possible in the world of movie magic.

I loved the challenge of turning the impossible into "reality," as we created things that only the imaginative minds of the writers could come up with.

We constructed a large container on wheels that was referred to as the Prop Box. Inside was a wealth of treasure and knowledge. Among the paraphernalia were such every day household items as wire, glue, nails, paint, tape, and a thousand other things.

But also in the box were the unusual: for example, colored "dragon breath," a hairpiece for a bald chimp, a bow tie and tuxedo for a praying mantis, a milking jar for poisonous snakes, a fake nose for a monkey, a tarantula's back scratcher, a spitting-cobra mask, nonfloat duck oil, and fake fangs for a toothless tiger . . . a cornucopia of illusion!

12

FLY AWAY

"I need 5,000 trained flies. Can you do it? Yes or no!" The voice at the other end of the phone was insistent.

"Well, I. . . ."

"Of course you can't, Helfer. *Nobody* can. Look, I told the director I'd make a couple of calls. So, now I have. The answer is obviously NO!"

"I *can* do it," I said, fitting my sentence neatly in between my caller's constant jabber, "but I'll need a couple of days."

The voice on the phone was silent a moment. Then: "You're kidding."

"No, really. Two days, and I'll be ready. What do they have to do?"

"There's this artificial, dead-looking 'thing' lying on the ground in the forest. The director wants thousands of flies to be crawling on it without flying away."

"Okay," I said. "Consider it done."

"No, wait. Then, he wants them *all* to fly away, on command—but not before."

"Okay, no problem," I said. "Two days."

"Wait. Did you hear what I said? They can't leave until he says okay. How are you going to keep them there, let alone have them fly away when he wants them to??"

"I'll stick each of their 20,000 legs in glue! Look, don't worry. Call me later, and I'll give you the figure. 'Bye."

127

Sometimes affection training was not the only answer. One could not "pet" a fly or earn its respect. I knew I would have to resort to the laws of nature for the answer to this one. I'd had the opportunity to work with various insects in the past. But *5,000!* I hoped I hadn't bitten off more than I could chew.

I went to work, first converting an old box in which we'd been keeping crickets (we raised them to feed to the tarantulas). The box was about three feet high by two feet square. Patching up a few holes, I scrubbed it clean, fixed a crooked door, and set it inside the snake room.

The next day I visited a good friend of mine, Professor Jonathan Ziller, an entomologist and researcher. His work area consisted of twenty to thirty lab-type cages made of fine-mesh wire. Each contained a different species of insect. Over a cup of coffee, I told him of my needs. We walked over to a cage that was being heated by a special infrared lamp. Inside I could see massive swarms of maggots—fly larvae, ready to be hatched into their next stage. As I stood there, the professor calculated the exact time when they would become flies. As his watch struck the "birthing" time, thousands of flies left their maggot bodies and were suddenly airborne, buzzing about the cage.

We both agreed that these flies, an unusually large type that resembled the horsefly, would be perfect. An added plus was the fact that they were all hybrid, incapable of breeding. Hence, in releasing them I would not be running the risk of upsetting the natural balance of the environment.

The professor gave me a batch of fly larvae, which he'd calculated would hatch on the morning of the shoot, along with a vial of a special, harmless tranquilizer in a gas capsule. The gas would be released when the tip of the cigarette-sized plastic tube was broken. With the vial set inside the fly box, all the flies could be put to sleep within seconds. Once the gas had dissipated in a matter of moments, the flies would awaken. The tranquilizer was, of course, harmless to people. A handshake later, I was off, gently carrying my brood with me.

On the morning of the shoot, all the flies hatched right on schedule. I loaded up and headed for the studio location. When

I arrived, I was greeted by a crew of disbelievers with tongue-in-cheek attitudes. Bets and jokes were being made in every direction, all in good-natured fun.

The director, a big, friendly sort, came over to me with a suspicious look in his eyes. "Is it true?"

"What?"

"That you can put 5,000 flies on something and they'll crawl around, but you can guarantee they won't fly right off?"

"It's true."

"Then when I tell you to let them go, they'll all fly away immediately?"

"Give or take a few."

"A few what?"

"Flies that won't fly away."

"If you pull this off, I'll double your fee," he said in disbelief.

"Ready whenever you are," I said, and headed for my fly house.

The camera was set. The "dead thing" turned out to be a special-effects monster baby that had supposedly died a while back and was now to be swarming with flies. Somebody was to walk by, and the flies would then have to fly away.

Everything was ready.

The skeptical assistant director yelled for the "fly man." One of my trainers and I carried the fly house over and set it near the camera. The loud buzzing of an enormous number of flies was obvious. Sheets of heavy paper prevented anyone from seeing into the box.

"Now, Ralph, I'll roll the camera whenever you say—okay?" asked the director.

"Sure, but everything has to be ready. I've only got 10,042 flies—just enough for two shots."

His look told me he wasn't sure whether I was putting him on or not.

"10,042—really!" he mumbled, and walked over to the camera.

With everything set, I opened the small door of the fly house. Hiding the gas capsule in the palm of my hand and reaching inside, I broke it open, closed the door, and waited for fifteen seconds. To everybody's amazement, the buzzing stopped. Next, I opened the door and scooped out three or four handfuls of flies. I shook them out as one would when counting a pound of peanuts. Putting the little sleeping flies all over the "body," I began to dramatically count the last few: "Five-thousand twenty, five-thousand twenty-one, five-thousand twenty-one . . . that makes it half!"

I told everyone to hold still, then I gave the flies a verbal cue: "Okay, guys—Jack, Bill, Mary—come on, up and at 'em!"

Slowly the flies started to awaken, then move around. In a few moments the whole mass of them was swarming all over the "thing," but they were still too drowsy to fly, as my professor friend had told me they would be.

"Okay, roll!" yelled the director. The camera rolled on the fly swarm, and I shot a look at the crew. They appeared to be in shock. Then, having gotten enough footage, the director shouted, "Okay, Ralph, *now!*"

My great moment.

"Okay, group," I said to the flies. "Get ready: on the count of three, all of you take off."

The crew, absolutely bug-eyed (forgive the pun), was hypnotized.

"One," I counted. They looked from the flies to me.

"Two."

"Three!" I yelled, clapping my hands and stamping my foot at the same time. Five thousand twenty-one flies flew up, up, around and around. The camera hummed until the director, rousing himself from his amazed state, said, "Cut!"

The entire crew was silent for a moment, and then they burst into applause and delighted laughter.

"You did it, you really did it!" said the director, slapping me heartily on the back. "I'm not even going to ask you how. I don't even want to know. But if I ever need a trained *anything,* you're the man I'll call!"

Straight-faced, I said, "Well, actually, I've recently trained 432 flies to form a chorus line on my arm, and on cue they all kick a leg at the same time."

The director, poker-faced, looked straight at me. "Which one?" he asked.

"Which one what?"

"Which leg?"

"The left one, of course!"

We all broke up laughing and headed home.

13

GERTRUDE'S JOURNEY

I was in Arizona for the shooting of the adventure film *Journey to the Center of the Earth,* starring James Mason, Pat Boone, and Arlene Dahl. The film was being shot in the fantastic Carlsbad Caverns, a mammoth network of caves spiraling down into the earth for two miles. The caves are renowned for their huge population of bats, millions upon millions of which darken the sky each night as they set out from the caves.

But the major drawback to working in the caves was not the bats but the cool temperature—a steady 58 degrees, winter or summer, day or night. Although not unpleasant at first, the chill and the dampness did, after a while, creep into one's flesh. We shot in the caves for six weeks. During that time, many of us never saw the light of day, since we went down into the caves before sunup and left after sundown.

I had been hired to supply the lead animal star, identified in the script as an eider duck named Gertrude. Now, eider ducks are not easy to come by, as they live in the northern part of Canada. The USDA insisted that a permit be issued before an eider duck could be allowed to enter the United States. Given that time was extremely short, I decided to "make" my own eider duck.

Through research I found out that eiders are generally pure white, with a dark ring around their eyes. Having worked on various films in which we had to color bird feathers (safely), I had my bird trainer bring me a few of the solid white tame ducks from our pond. They were fairly manageable, as they had been hatched and raised by the staff. We went to work immediately.

First, we carefully washed each duck's head with a mild detergent to remove the natural oils from the feathers. Next, using a special vegetable-dye paint and a small paintbrush, we painted a very delicate ring around each eye. Because each animal star needs several doubles, we painted a total of four "Gertrudes."

Once the paint had dried and the natural oils had returned (within a few days), the rings around the eyes looked quite realistic. In fact, I believe it would have taken a top ornithologist to tell the difference between *our* eider ducks and the real McCoy!

After completing the training, we headed for Arizona. I was, of course, teased a lot for "training" a duck. It's true that after handling lions, tigers, and elephants, working with birds was a bit different, but I care for *all* animals. Plus, I was looking forward to seeing the caves.

I was up and ready to work early that first morning, anxious to introduce the ducks to their new environment. Upon arriving at the caves, I was amazed at the size of the entrance. It was an awesome, huge cavern of seemingly endless space and darkness. Down in the main cave, one could imagine seeing etched in the cold walls such shapes as old sailing vessels, spaceships, skyscrapers, faces, and gargoyles. We were working in a magical spot called the King's Chambers. Mammoth stalagmites and stalactites shone in the darkness. The huge, brute arc lights burned a hole in the abyss, but the darkness seemed to eat the light.

After meeting the director and crew, I opened the portable cage, and out waddled Gertrude and her friends. Quack! Quack! The ducks' quacking reverberated throughout the caves. The sound man came over and asked if the duck always quacked.

"You've got to be kidding," I said. "I mean, *everybody* knows that ducks quack!"

He told me that either the quack went or the ducks went, because the high-pitched sound echoed in the caves and would destroy the soundtrack. I *had* noticed that a person whispering on one side of the cave could easily be heard on the far side, 200 yards away. What to do? The director wanted the duck, but it looked as though he might have to do without it.

I was having dinner that evening with some of the crew and cast when Pat Boone walked up. He must have noticed my glum mood, because he asked me, "What's wrong? Food no good?"

"The food's great," I mumbled back.

"Well, what else, then?" the velvet voice asked back.

"We're going home," I said. "Gertrude, her buddies, and me." Pat looked surprised. "Why, old Gertrude was great!"

"But she quacks," I said.

"Well, I should hope so! Most ducks *do,* you know," he exclaimed.

A light bulb went on in my head. "*Most* do," I repeated. "But not *all!*" I jumped up from the table, almost knocking the salad over. "Thanks, Pat," I said. "I think you've just saved the day!"

I called the ranch. "Toni, emergency! Grab four of the Muscovy mix, and the vegetable dye. Hop on a plane, and be here tonight."

As soon as Toni arrived, we went to work. We put the ducks in a tub of warm water and cleaned off all the barnyard debris with which they were encrusted. Once their brilliant white color had reappeared, we applied dishwasher detergent to remove their natural oils. Finally, we added the black rings around their eyes. By 2:00 A.M. the ducks were huddled in a towel, lying in a row, with a heater blowing warm, dry air over them.

By morning they were dry. They looked great, and although they weren't as trained as Gertrude and her friends, they didn't quack. The reason: Muscovy ducks are quackless! Although these ducks are usually multicolored, ours had bred with our "Gertrude ducks," and the result had been pure-white, quackless ducks. Hence, our new movie stars!

The next day, when the sound man discovered that no sound came out when the ducks opened their beaks, he looked at me suspiciously.

"What did you do?" he asked.

"I took care of the problem," I said, menacingly.

He looked at me, cocking one eyebrow, and said, "You beast! How *could* you?"

"It was easy," I said in my best Bogart voice.

He walked away, looking as though he felt guilty about having been the one who'd caused the ducks to go through such agony and pain.

✹

According to the script, the duck was supposed to ride on the shoulder or in the backpack of the young costar, who told me that this was his first film. When I arrived, I told the young man that we would have to pretrain so the birds could get used to him. We started by having him carry the duck in his arm. A look of shock crossed his face when "Gertrude II" relieved herself in his hand. Things only got worse after that. When I put her on his shoulder, she sat there, perched like an eagle—and then, puffing her feathers, she proceeded to eliminate down his back. He stormed out, yelling something about how our training should have included a cork! Gertrude II definitely had him pegged.

A meeting with the director gave us no solution. The actor simply refused to work with the duck. As we were talking, Arlene Dahl walked up and began to talk to and pet Gertrude II. When she asked to hold her, I obliged. Arlene sat down, and I gently rested Gertrude in her arms. Everybody stopped talking and looked at each other, afraid to breathe.

"I like her—she's cute," she said, flashing her gorgeous smile.

We waited, but nothing happened. Gertrude II, looking up at Arlene, cuddled up in her lap and proceeded to preen herself. We all took a deep breath.

"Would you like to have her as your buddy . . . I mean, in the film?" asked the director nervously.

"Sure—I'd love to!" she said.

And that was that! Arlene and Gertrude II became inseparable. At the end of the movie, when Gertrude II was "killed," the situation leading up to her "death" seemed so real that we all felt the loss.

One day I was sitting with the crew during the shoot when the young costar came over and joined us.

"Boy, am I glad to be rid of that bag of feathers!" he said.

An old-timer in the business looked up at him and said, "You're foolish, young fella."

"What do you mean?"

"Don't you understand why she took the duck?"

"She likes birds, that's all."

"Oh, she likes birds, all right. But any seasoned performer knows that finding a reason to be near an animal star gives you more exposure in a movie. Whenever the camera is on the duck, it's also on Arlene. Don't you realize that she'll probably be on camera twice as much with the duck than without? I would have thought that a new actor such as yourself would have needed all the exposure you could get!"

The actor got up and, dusting off his new trousers, said, "Well, I guess I blew it." He walked away, dejected.

Gertrude II and her entourage enjoyed working in the caves, and they actually seemed to relish the cool temperatures. It wasn't unusual to see them swimming in the ice-cold underground ponds.

As for the sound man, it wasn't until the end of the movie that he learned I had exchanged the first ducks for a quackless type.

When the crew finally let him in on it, the only response he could come up with was, "Speechless!"

14

"RABBIT MAN"

"Okay, Rabbit Man . . ."—God, how we all hated to be called that—we *did* have names!— ". . . when I tell you, release the rabbit, and make him run across the set."

Years ago, people who worked any animal in the film or TV industries were called by the name of that animal. In this case, the assistant director was referring to a young fellow, an amateur trainer who was working a rabbit. I was there as the "Cat Man," working a cougar. We were filming a spaghetti Western on a back lot in Hollywood. The filmmakers had poured tons of beach sand over the asphalt, planted a bunch of cacti, and thrown a few rocks around. When seen from above it looked like the middle of a Western desert.

"Roll camera!" The Rabbit Man petted the rabbit, then touched his cheek to the soft fur. I heard him whisper, "Okay now, Pinky—be a star!"

"Action!"

The trainer released the rabbit and sprang back as though he were releasing a greyhound. The rabbit, however, hopped two feet away and proceeded to nibble on nearby brush.

"Cut! What the - - is this?! He's got to *run*, man! *Run!*"

"But I told you, dyeing his fur doesn't make him a jackrabbit. He's just my son's pet. . . ."

"Give him here!" interrupted a heavyset man with a gravelly voice. He yanked the rabbit from the trainer by its ears, then shot a look at the director. "Get ready to roll!" he grunted.

The inexperienced trainer followed the burly man. "Hey! He's *my* rabbit!"

"Look, son, if you want to work in this business again, just lay back and let an 'old boy' show you how it's done."

I left my caged cougar in the hands of Jack Durkin, my assistant, and walked over to see what the "old boy" had in mind. He unlocked the door of his large prop box. Inside were hundreds of miscellaneous things, hanging or piled up. The man reached in and took out an electric shaver. He plugged it in and proceeded to shave the rabbit's hind end. Then he took a five-gallon can of some sort of liquid and poured a small amount into a bottle. Finally, he yanked a piece of cotton from a jar and grabbed a piece of sandpaper. Scooping the rabbit up under his arm, he headed back to the set. The trainer followed humbly.

"Okay, we're ready," the man said, addressing the director.

"Wait a minute!" I butted in. "You can't do that!" I knew by the smell of the liquid what the prop man had in mind.

"Who are you?" asked the assistant director (A/D).

Facetiously, I said, "I'm the Cat Man."

"So? What's your problem? When we need the cougar, we'll call you."

"My 'problem' is what the prop man is going to do to the rabbit to make him run!"

The A/D was a bit agitated. Turning to the prop man, he asked, "What *are* you going to do?"

"I've just got some stuff to make the rabbit run," he said innocently.

"It's turpentine!" I shouted in a rather loud voice. "He's going to put it on the rabbit's shaved rear end after he's rubbed it raw with sandpaper!"

"Will it show?" asked the A/D, talking through a locked jaw.

"Will what show?"

"The spot that was shaved. I don't want to ruin the shot!" he yelled. He looked directly at me with contempt.

I fumed. "What about the pain the rabbit will suffer?"

"Look, Mr. Humane Society, rabbits get killed every day," said the A/D. "We *eat* rabbits! Today's shooting is costing $20,000, and you're upping our budget every minute! Now, let's go! Hit the lights, Jack!"

140

Across the set on a stool sat an aging humane officer from the local organization. He was whittling away on a chunk of wood. I walked over to him. "Aren't you going to do something? You heard what's going on."

He looked up at me with weary eyes and sighed deeply. Turning his rather heavy waistline toward the scene, he grumbled hoarsely, "Wait a minute, Gary. I have to make a formal complaint regarding what you're about to do."

"So noted, Chris!" yelled the A/D. "Okay, roll camera!"

Chris went back to his whittling. The rabbit trainer sat nearby, scrunched down against a bunch of artificial cacti.

"Action!" yelled the director. The prop man rasped the sandpaper across the shaved area on the rabbit's rear. He then poured the turpentine into the cotton and wiped it into the raw skin, burning the animal severely. The rabbit kicked so hard that I thought he'd break his neck. The prop man dropped the cotton and, holding the rabbit tight, headed him in the proper direction and let go. The rabbit went crazy. He shot across the sand at lightning speed. Then he crashed into a bush, sprang into the air, fell backward, and hit hard against a rock. He was knocked out, and there was blood dripping from his skull. It all happened in a matter of seconds.

"Cut! Cut! We got it! Someone catch the rabbit! Next setup is down the road." And as the director walked away, I heard him say, "I just needed the run so we can cut before he hits the rock."

A few of the crew remained behind to see how the rabbit was. We picked him up and washed off the blood and turpentine, but it was too late. Pinky was dead. He had never recovered from the blow to the head.

The set emptied quickly. I walked over to the humane officer. "Why didn't you do something? It's your job!"

"I did all I can," he said. "But we don't really have any power. The most we can do is put some money in the telephone and call the police."

"Well, anybody can do that," I said.

"Exactly—and the police would have to get authority to enter private property. By then, the crew would have moved on to another set, and the worst they'd get is a slap on the wrist or a verbal reprimand. Then I'd be out of a job, 'cause I was a troublemaker—and at my age, jobs are hard to come by."

I turned to go. The rabbit trainer laid his dead charge in a pretty-colored crate marked "Pinky." As he left, I heard him murmur something about what he was going to tell his son.

15

A HANDFUL OF TAILS

In addition to the thousands of movie and television appearances that our animals made, we supplied creatures "great and small" for countless commercials.

The calls usually went something like this. The phone would ring in the late afternoon, and a frantic voice—usually that of someone calling long-distance from New York—would spill out some request they thought was probably crazy. For example: "We need a lion to walk down the street and go down into the subway. And by the way, there are people everywhere."

This was typical of what was called for when we did the Dreyfus commercials. Zamba, who was not only beautiful but also easy to work with, was the animal most often called upon for such assignments. Zamba loved milk, so when a studio called for a lion to drink some milk out of a bowl with a kitten, Zamba was the obvious choice.

"Okay, Toni," I said, "put the kitty by the bowl of milk! That's right. Easy does it."

The kitten immediately started to lap up the milk.

"Okay, now I'll turn Zamba loose. Ready?"

"Ready!" Toni yelled back.

I undid the clip on Zamba's neck and let him go. He headed straight for the milk. Sticking his huge nose into the bowl, he began to lap up the contents. The kitten, caught in a small tidal wave of milk, held his ground, was determined to get his share. Zamba cleaned the bowl, licked his chops, and gave a little nudge to the kitten that set him back on his haunches. Then he left the set, circled the floor a few times, and flopped down—and was snoring within thirty seconds.

Zamba's miraculously mild disposition was due mainly to the affection training he'd received from us since he was a mere cub. Having spent hours in our house—sleeping in bed with us, eating in the kitchen when we did, and keeping me company in the evenings—he was more of a true friend than were some of the humans I'd encountered during my work in Hollywood.

Zamba's diet also contributed to his gentleness. Having been brought up for a period of time as a partial vegetarian, he was quite used to dairy products and vegetables, since we often fed him milk, large "cakes" of cheese, eggs, beans, carrots, and potatoes, with only a touch of chicken thrown in. I believe that many meat-eating animals can thrive on full or partial vegetarian diets; Zamba was a prime example. I also feel that if this diet were continued for some period of time, the carnivores' aggressive nature would diminish considerably, though the change could take many generations. Although I am not an advocate of turning all meat-eaters into complete vegetarians, I feel that the idea does create some interesting possibilities.

❋

One of my trainers rushed into the house.

"Sorry to bother you, Ralph, but there's no way I'm going to put hair curlers in a lion's mane!"

"Why?" I asked. That morning a representative of the Toni home permanents had called, asking whether we could give a lion a permanent wave for an advertisement, to show that the treatment was so good it could even curl a lion's mane!

" 'Cause that's woman stuff!" he replied, looking down at his shuffling feet.

"Okay, look: how about if you control the lion and Tana does the perm?"

He agreed to that, and within an hour we had Simba, one of our adult male African lions, out on the lawn. Tana was soon shampooing his mane, giving him the appearance of a giant drowned rat. The trainer held the leash while Simba tried to lick off the suds. After hosing off the soap, Tana put dozens of rollers in Simba's mane, applied the setting solution, and then waited for it to set.

Simba kept trying to roll over and rub the curlers off, but we convinced him otherwise by occasionally offering him a bit of his favorite treat, cottage cheese.

The end result was spectacular! Simba's mane looked huge. Massive ringlets covered his shoulders and neck and hung over his face.

For the next lion call that came in, we had to use another lion. The client would never have understood why a lion had curls, and I was not about to explain!

✳

As the Schlitz bull, Zane had been a famous commercial animal for a long time, and we enjoyed working with him as much as he enjoyed the work. One of the most interesting stories about Zane is how we acquired him.

I was sitting on a corral fence one day with a bunch of studio people, chatting about the movie industry. Below us were twelve or fourteen huge Brahma bulls. Some were mixed with other breeds and were of different colors, sizes, and shapes, but there was one thing they all had in common—they were all *mean!* If anybody fell into that arena, he would have been instantly gored, trampled, or rammed up against the bars of the fence, or possibly all three.

A rather small, elderly wrangler, wearing baggy jeans held up by a Western belt with an oversized silver buckle, a ragged Western shirt, and cowboy boots complete with rusty spurs, was talking shop with us. The drawstring from a bag of Bull Durham tobacco hung from his shirt pocket.

"Ya wanna see me ride one?" We all stopped talking and looked at him.

"What did you say?" someone asked. Again he said that he could ride one of the bulls. Three or four of us chuckled.

145

"How do you propose to do that?" someone asked.

"Put some money down, and I'll show ya."

"How much?" we all chorused.

"Well, I don't know." The old wrangler took off his hat. "I'll tell you when it feels right," he said, shaking the hat.

"You mean you'll really go in there with those killers and jump up on one of their backs?!" I asked.

"Yep!"

"You're crazy!" someone exclaimed.

The old man handed his empty hat to the nearest man.

"Okay! I'm in," said the man, dropping in a five-spot.

"Me, too!" said another.

Pretty soon everybody was tossing money into the hat and passing it on. When the hat was handed back to him, the old wrangler looked at it, took out the coins and returned them to their owners, crunched the bills down into the crown of the hat, and then deftly put it on his head without spilling a buck.

He jumped down off the fence and started walking around the outside, looking at the bulls. Some of the animals snorted and grunted; others just stood there, quivering to get rid of the flies.

Then the wrangler jumped up on the fence and, without a second's hesitation, threw himself into the arena! A huge bull pawed the ground, lowered his terrifying horns, and almost literally flew at the gutsy little guy. In one jump, the wrangler cleared the bull's horns and scampered up the corral fence. He must have been eight feet up on the fence, and yet the horn just missed him! These rodeo bulls, weighing 2,000 pounds and standing six feet at the shoulder, were serious. Now we were really worried for him.

"Look, buddy! Keep the money!! Okay, gang?" someone called out anxiously. A chorus of agreement followed—"Yeah!" "Sure!" "You can stop now!" But without saying a word himself, the old wrangler dropped down on the outside and again started walking around the perimeter. His eyes were as sharp as flint as he surveyed the bulls.

"This guy is gonna get *killed!*" someone said.

"We've got to stop him!" said someone else. But we were too hypnotized, too engrossed with what was happening, to stop him.

The wrangler halted, waiting. Then he leaped up onto the fence, and again dropped quietly into the arena. This time, bold as a lion, he walked directly toward a giant bull. We were afraid to breathe. Reaching the animal, he grabbed hold of a tuft of hair that was growing out of the hump on its neck. Then he stepped back, and with a short run, a jump, and a scramble, he was *up!* The bull walked a few yards, and stopped.

Triumphantly, the old man took off his hat and, cupping it in his arms, bowed to us! A quick flip and the hat was back on his head. Then he threw a leg over and was off the bull and heading toward the fence.

A moment later we were gathered around him, cheering. The little man smiled, tipped his hat forward graciously, and walked off.

One of us yelled after him, "How did you do it?"

The wrangler glanced around and gave us a big smile and a wink, but he just kept walking.

It wasn't long after this that a man came to my ranch looking for work, driving up in a closed-in double horse trailer. He told me he had done studio work in the past and was looking for anything involving horses, cattle, and livestock. I suddenly recognized him as the same man who had done the miraculous bull stunt.

"How in the world did you ever do that?" I asked him. He looked at me for a while, and with the same smile he'd given us that day, said, "Do I work?"

I looked at this brave old tiger and replied, "Sure," knowing that hiring him would also bring me an answer to my question.

He turned around and went to his trailer, took a halter and a lead rope out of the cab, and walked around to the back door of the trailer. Then he pulled the tailgate down and disappeared inside. I heard some commotion, and out stepped an enormous Brahma bull! The old-timer walked the bull over to me as though it were a puppy. I stared at both of them.

"How did you *do* it?" I asked him again.

"He's neutered!" said the old wrangler. "If you neuter them early enough and work real hard, these great old animals are as gentle as lambs."

147

I stared in amazement.

"But he doesn't *look* neutered!"

"Well, there's a special way of taking the testicles out and leaving the sac," he said. "Makes 'em look like any other bull."

"It sure does!" I said.

I knew now why he had kept walking around the arena: he had been trying to line up *his* bull so he didn't have to get near the others. Once the bull was in a favorable position, it was a simple matter to go in and get up on him.

The Schlitz company used this Brahma bull, Zane, to represent their beer. In one commercial, Zane was used as a gentle beast, carrying a person on his back as he meandered down a city street. Another time, he walked carefully through a shop full of delicate glass and porcelain. Whatever the job, Zane proved to be outstanding. Although his hump and massive horns gave him a ferocious look, he was an agreeable and lovable animal.

*

Some of the most rewarding commercials we were ever asked to do were for the Hartford Insurance Company, whose logo was an elk standing on a mountain. It was a huge, mature, fully racked elk, and we were asked to obtain one just like it.

At that time we had some tame deer in our collection, but none were anywhere near the size of the elk depicted in the logo, nor did they have its majestic quality. Could we get one? We doubted if we would be fortunate enough to find a tame one, because elks are noted for being dangerous. However, we started a search of all the zoos and animal compounds in the United States and Canada. In the process, we discovered that there was a type of deer that resembled an elk. In fact, after a close look at the logo, many felt that the animal pictured wasn't an elk at all but a European red deer.

Although many calls came in offering various types of deer and elk, there was only one that intrigued me. This was a call from a small zoo in Florida. We flew down there and found that the animal *was,* in fact, a large eight-pointer. He was heavy in body, with a thick, reddish coat, and he appeared to weigh at least 500 pounds. He so strongly resembled the elk in the logo that we decided he would be the perfect animal to represent Hartford Insurance. We transported him back to California and put him in a large open pen to give him as much room as possible.

We knew that the only way we could successfully work Lawrence, as we called him, would be with the reward system. Although he would allow us to pet him, he would not tolerate a leash of any kind. Yet he had to be controlled somehow, since the company planned to shoot the commercials in the mountains, and we didn't want to lose him.

Lawrence showed a desire to be with people. I assigned my trainer Steve to be his head trainer. Because of his quiet and patient manner, Steve was well suited for the job. Around the outside perimeter we rigged what is referred to as a "hot line," a thin wire approved by the Humane Society to keep animals in or out of a particular area. When an animal contacts the wire, it feels a small electric shock—just enough to persuade it to make a change of direction. Steve had Lawrence broken to the hot line in no time.

Our biggest fear was that Lawrence would "drop" his horns before the commercials could be shot. All members of the deer family, including moose and elk, lose their horns every year. As the spring breeding time comes around, new horns sprout through, always a little bit bigger than the horns of the previous year. They emerge with a velvetlike cover, which is eventually scraped off as the animal fights with other males or rubs its horns against trees and bushes. (Animal behaviorists say that animals in this stage are "in velvet.")

Lawrence looked beautiful up there in Southern California's Angeles Crest mountains. The landscape glowed with the deep green of late spring. We had rigged our hot line for many acres, forming a huge circle through the pine forest. But not once did Lawrence ever test the wire or try to escape.

There have been times when we have had to separate the concepts of "affection" and "training." To get Lawrence to perform required very little training, since he was not required to

149

do anything that wasn't natural for him. The only difficulty was in getting him to do it at a particular time and place! So "affection" became the key.

For the first scene, the director wanted Lawrence to come up the hill, stop at a certain spot and look out over the valley, then move on. Using Lawrence's favorite oat and barley mix, we coaxed him into a corral, out of view of the camera. I stationed four of my handlers along his designated path.

When the director yelled for action and the camera rolled, we opened the corral. A handler situated near the camera called out to Lawrence, who by now knew his name and responded to it. At the same time the man shook a bucket of grain. Upon hearing this, Lawrence started up the hill, looking quite natural. At the point at which he was supposed to stop, a handler carrying a large sheet of metal sprang up out of the forest some 100 yards away and raced across an open area, beating the sheet with a stick. Lawrence stopped his walk and glanced up at the silly commotion, with a look that was exactly what the director wanted—proud and noble. Then, having satisfied his curiosity, he resumed his walk and vanished over the hill, to the sound of yet another bucket of grain persistently rasping out an invitation for him.

Our affection paid off. The weeks and months of petting, brushing, hand-feeding, and gentle handling were just what was needed to get all of the scenes shot. If the director had asked for anything unnatural (such as Lawrence's wearing a hat or bowing), we would never have been able to produce it—at least not in the short amount of time we'd been given.

Lawrence did eventually lose his horns, but not before we had finished all of the commercials that were asked of us. The Hartford people signed us to a contract to do many, many commercials with them in the following years involving Lawrence. Some required him to walk down a residential street, while others had him walk up and watch while a house was being constructed.

One crisp morning while on location, I walked out into the forest and stood behind a bush, watching Lawrence. He was nibbling on a small patch of grass. I approached quietly so as not to bother him. He must have sensed my presence, for all of a sudden he raised his head and stood perfectly still, looking out into the forest. Each muscle was tense. He could feel me, but he couldn't see me.

For a moment he seemed to be invisible, blending into the natural background of the forest. His horns became the branches of trees, his body the bushes and the earth itself. Lawrence stood omnipotent. He *was* the forest.

My mind hurtled back to a time in my boyhood when my uncle, an avid hunter, dragged me out into the woods one morning to accompany him on a hunt. For what seemed like hours we walked silently, stopping occasionally to scan the forest for movement of any kind.

Suddenly, in a clearing, we came upon a magnificent buck. Grabbing me by the shoulder, my uncle pulled me down so that we were crouching out of sight behind a bush. He thrust the rifle into my hands, whispering harshly, "Shoot him! Shoot him!"

I gazed at the deer through the rifle sight. The deer looked up. He seemed to be looking directly at me with his gentle brown eyes. For a moment, I envisioned the bullet striking his chest, his body crumbling to the ground, blood gushing.

I lowered the gun. . . .

My thoughts brought me back to the present. I stepped out into the open so Lawrence could see me clearly. He whipped his head around and stared at me for a long time. Then his body relaxed, and he went back to eating. As I walked away, I knew for certain that I had made the right choice long ago.

PART V

HOLLYWOOD'S
WILD LIFE

When people say they've "made it," it usually just means that they've acquired a great deal of money. In terms of my own success, "making it" has meant more than just financial rewards. It's meant the knowledge I've gained, the people I've met, and the places I've seen. Most important, it has meant the contribution I've made to enhancing communication between man and animal.

One of the benefits of working in the film industry is that it has brought me into contact with some of the most famous people in the world. Often, our meetings would occur in strange places or under unique circumstances. I met Kirk Douglas when I had to throw a rattlesnake in his face; Shirley Temple, when my baby alligator bit her finger; and Danny Kaye, while working a lion in an arena.

What a great thrill it was to introduce my animal movie stars to the two-footed ones. Of course, some of the human stars couldn't stand the "dirty creatures," and others were jealous of their involvement in the films. But most seemed to feel a sense of true warmth and excitement on meeting their wild counterparts.

Many of the celebrities I've met have been natural animal lovers. Included among these are Brooke Shields, Burt Lancaster, Sonny and Cher, Clint Eastwood, Bo and John Derek, Bill Holden, Stefanie Powers, Pat Boone, Carol Burnett, Betty White, Robert Mitchum, and Walt Disney.

One of the most special moments in my career occurred on the day that Johnny Weissmuller, the greatest Tarzan of them all, came out to the ranch to work with some of my elephants for a film he was doing. He was very impressed with our training methods. "If only we'd had the benefit of your affection-trained animals in the old days, Ralph," he said, "our films would have been a lot better, safer, and a hell of a lot more fun!"

16

MOVIE STARS

When an exotic animal is brought into civilization, it is confronted with an environment that is totally different from anything it has encountered in the past. This is particularly true for an animal brought onto a movie set, where it has to cope not only with the real world, but also with a fantasy world in which anything the imagination can concoct can happen.

All animals, even affection-trained ones, can be dangerous. They all have the potential of doing damage to humans and other animals. Animals in the wild will attack if their young are in danger, if they themselves are threatened, or if they are hungry and need food. This is an instinctive reaction, and any naturalist can see it coming.

Bringing an exotic animal into civilization introduces it to a whole new set of situations. The "old-timers" among the animal stars—those that have worked in the business most of their lives—can usually handle the unexpected with a casual attitude. Not surprisingly, they're worth their weight in gold to filmmakers.

Animals unaccustomed to such situations are a different story. While in a way the film business is the best training ground available, using animals in films can put not only the animals but also the actors and crews at risk.

You can have the best-trained animal in the world, until it steps on a bare electrical wire. The unexpected shock can cause the animal to react with hostility. He may hold you responsible, or he may jump into your arms for protection!

The bursting of a large klieg light bulb is enough to scare *me* for a moment; what must it do to a tiger, who's probably never heard such a thing?

Then there's the smell of gunpowder wafting from the back lot where a Western is being shot. Or maybe a huge elephant from another set walks by.

And what about accidents, such as an animal's stepping on a tack, or a crew member's hot coffee getting spilled on an animal? What if the script says a lion has to walk by a table prepared with a full dinner, including a roast turkey and a stuffed pig? The list of potentially dangerous situations is endless.

It was no surprise when Bandit, our star raccoon, panicked when a large fake tree toppled to the ground with a crash that resounded from one end of the sound stage to the other.

"Do you see him?" I yelled, squeezing through a thick forest of two-by-four wooden struts, heavy beams, spiderwebs, and dust.

"I think he's over here!" Marilyn Monroe's voice echoed through the maze. I found her on the floor on her hands and knees, trying to talk Bandit out of his hiding place.

We were at the Twentieth Century–Fox studios, filming *The River of No Return* on one of the giant indoor stages. To create a massive artificial forest, the studio had had some 200 adult pine trees hauled in and secured to the platform we were now under. The ground was strewn with leaves and branches; looming in the distance were snow-capped "mountains," painted on the giant canvas walls.

"Come on, Bandit. Nobody is going to hurt you," Marilyn coaxed. "He was doing great until that tree fell over. It scared him half to death, I think."

I joined Marilyn on the floor, and we crawled forward until we could see the raccoon. He had taken refuge up in the support structure, and it appeared that there was no way he was going to come out until he wanted to.

The crew stood around, waiting for us to retrieve Bandit. The brute lights were shut down. One big klieg light, left on for the workers to continue their chores, cast an eerie green light throughout the structure.

"Are you okay, Miss Monroe?" a voice called from somewhere.

"Yes, fine," she answered.

"Should we come in?" another voice bellowed.

"No, I don't think so," I said. "Too many people would just scare him more. Just give us a little time. He'll come out."

Marilyn called to Bandit again. We had crawled as far as we could go, and the hard floor was taking its toll on our knees and elbows.

"The director is really going to be mad," I said. "I hear it's costing $40,000 per day to shoot this film."

"Yeah, I know," she said.

I looked over at her. She had a big grin on her face. We broke up laughing.

"You like animals?" I asked her.

"I love animals, especially horses. I love wild animals, too. You've always liked animals?"

I nodded. "More than people!"

"I know what you mean," she said. "I always wonder what animals are thinking. They're perfect, you know? I wonder why they're perfect, and we're not. I mean, we *are* supposed to be the intelligent ones, right?"

Suddenly shifting position, she cried, "Hey, look!"

Bandit had come out of his hiding place and was on his way up Marilyn's legs. We sat up carefully. Bandit seemed to be his old self again. I put his little collar on him and snapped the leash.

"We got him!" I yelled.

There was instant reaction from all around. Lights snapped on, shadows moved, voices called out. "Okay, folks, picture time! Wardrobe, stand ready! Second team, please!"

Marilyn and I crawled out of the two-by-four jungle. It was good to stand up again! Marilyn was immediately inundated by the team of people who would be getting her ready for the next shot. Her costar, Robert Mitchum, gave me a wink and a thumbs-up. I smiled back, dusting my pants off. Bandit jumped up in my arms, and I turned to go.

"See you, Marilyn!" I called.
"See you, Ralph! 'Bye, Bandit!"

✱

In my early days, reptiles were a specialty of mine. I had a collection of rattlesnakes, pythons, and boa constrictors, all kept in the family apartment. Even though some of the pythons and boas were up to twenty-four feet long and weighed close to 250 pounds, they were easy to house in boxes in our small apartment, thus enabling me to own enough of a collection to get my start in the film business. In addition to the reptiles, I also had tarantulas, scorpions, centipedes, millipedes, preying mantises, and other colorful oddities.

To find the rattlers, harmless snakes, and lizards, friends and I would go collecting in the Hollywood hills. One of my favorite companions on these ventures was a neighbor, a lanky, personable teenager named Carol, whose burning ambition was to work in the film business as an actress. The Burnetts lived in the same building as I did, and Carol and I spent many a day hiking and talking and sharing our dreams. I was thrilled when Carol made it, becoming internationally known and loved.

The snake for which I received the most calls was the cobra. These beautiful creatures, six to eight feet in length, would willingly rear their heads for most of the shots we needed. Whenever the script called for a poisonous snake to work with a performing artist, it was our obligation to render the snake temporarily harmless. Transforming a lethal reptile into a safe "actor" is a simple procedure, completely humane for the animal.

First, the snake is milked of its venom. This is done by first covering a glass vial with a thin piece of stretched rubber. The snake's head is grasped carefully after it has been pinned down with a "snake stick." When the snake's mouth is pushed against the rim of the vial, the reptile will attempt to bite, and the exposed fangs will pierce the rubber. Pressure from the trainer's fingers causes venom to be spewed into the vial.

Often, the trainer also massages the glands at the back of the snake's head to cause more venom to be ejected. Once milking has been done, the venom is carefully packaged and sent on to institutions that use it to develop antivenin and for cancer research.

Next, the fangs are extracted. This causes no pain to the animal, and new fangs can appear within twenty-four hours. (With many reptiles, great care must be taken in extracting the fangs, because others lie ready to take their place. In some cases we have had to remove two or three fangs from *each* side of a snake's jaw!) Finally, a mild local tranquilizer is given, and the snake's jaws are sutured shut. For the time being, the snake is quite harmless and can be handled without worry.

After filming, the sutures are removed, and the venom comes back immediately.

I once had to work a cobra with Lana Turner and Richard Burton in a film called *Rains of Ranchipur.* In the scene, which was supposed to take place at night, Lana was to wander away from the safety of the campfire and encounter a cobra, which would prepare to strike. Upon hearing her scream, Burton was to grab a firebrand and, racing to her side, throw it at the snake. To reassure them, I had shown them both how we extracted the fangs and the poison to render the snake harmless for the shot. Neither one seemed worried.

However, the insurance company felt differently! On the morning of the shot, a special truck arrived in the wooded area that was to serve as the location. In the truck was an enormous piece of glass, a full inch thick, ten feet long, and six feet high! It was so heavy that it took a crane to lift it off the truck, and many men to move it into position.

The insurance company representatives stated that they were not allowed to let the shot take place unless the glass was used. The extent to which the company had gone was truly laughable. The glass was strong enough to hold back an elephant! In any case, after many hours of adjustment, the glass was in position and secure. I think the actors were more afraid of the glass falling over on them than they were of being harmed by the cobra! I then positioned the snake on one side of the glass; Richard and Lana were on the other.

Initially, the cobra was covered; when working with poisonous snakes or snakes that are extremely active, we always put something over them, such as a box or a blanket, to keep them calm and in one spot before the shot is taken. Otherwise, reptiles have a tendency to crawl away or to perform before the camera is ready.

When everyone was in position, the director yelled "Action," and I reached in and pulled off the bag that I had placed over the cobra. Instantly, the snake reared up some three feet in the air, spread a beautiful hood, and kept his eyes on me. To the camera, the snake appeared to be staring directly at Lana. She came into the scene, saw the cobra, and screamed. Richard got the firebrand and hurled it at the snake (a close-up of a fake snake was used to show the "cobra" being struck by the firebrand and knocked away). The director yelled "Cut!" We'd gotten it on the first take!

I thought it was quite fitting when, after the shot, the insurance agent forgot that the piece of glass was there and walked straight into it, getting quite a bump on his head! I wonder who *he* sued?!

✳

Although shooting on a Hollywood set with exotic animals can pose all sorts of difficulties, when it comes to facing the unpredictable, nothing compares to shooting on location in a foreign country. A film crew can be faced with mind-boggling challenges, from language problems to unseasonable weather.

Such was the experience I shared with Bill Holden. Bill, who was known for being a lover of nature and all its animals, became one of my most treasured friends. We met in Kenya in 1960, during filming of *The Lion*. Being a partner in the world-famous Mount Kenya Safari Club gave Bill the opportunity to spend a considerable amount of time in a country he had grown to love. The many safaris and film locations we shared took us to some of the most scenic areas in Kenya. But, for sheer delight and comfort, the club stood at the top. I have many fond memories of happenings at the club involving the animals I was keeping there during filming.

One night, Bill, Capucine (Bill's female costar in this particular film), my assistant, Stuart, and I were all enjoying a "sundowner" when I suggested to Stuart that he look in on the lions before it got too late. Twentieth Century–Fox had had an animal compound built on the grounds of the club, below the swimming pool and just at the edge of the forest. Stuart, a six-foot, six-inch Englishman who was fairly new to our company, took a flashlight and headed down toward the cats. About ten minutes later, the apartment door was thrown open, and there stood Stuart—clothes askew, eyes wide, hair a mess. We all jumped up.

"Stuart, what in the world . . . ?" I sat him down on the edge of the bed. "What happened?"

Bill poured him a drink to help settle his nerves.

"Well," Stuart began, "I headed down across the lawn and cut into the old dirt road toward the forest. I found the trail all right, and flipped on the torch [flashlight]. It's pretty dark in there, you know."

His breath was coming a little more evenly.

"And then I rounded a bend, and standing there was one of the lions. It was a bit too dark to see whether it was Zamba or Junior, so I yelled at him, running as I went—'What the bloody hell are you doing out here? Somebody left the lock undone, didn't they!?' The lion took off as I got within a couple of yards of him, and disappeared in the dark. I ran the rest of the way to the compound, afraid that *all* of the lions had gotten out." He paused.

"So what happened?" Bill yelled.

"They were all there!!! All three of them. The locks were bolted. They had never left!"

"You mean . . ." Bill, started "that the lion you yelled at and ran after was *wild?*

Stuart nodded. "I didn't want to leave the compound and come back on that dark path, but . . . I did! I don't remember touching the ground till I arrived here!!"

Stuart's experience is talked about even now by the old-timers at the club, in the evening around the bar. Stuart went on to become one of the best directors in Hollywood, and he still laughs about that night.

❋

Our stay in Kenya was lengthened by a freak rainy season. It rained nonstop for three months. Rivers overflowed their banks, bridges washed out, and filming was brought to an abrupt halt.

Most of our days were spent hoping the sun would reappear. After a couple of weeks, Trevor Howard, Bill's other costar, suggested that we ease our way out of the club and take the Land Rover to Nanyuki, a small town ten miles away, for a bit of fun.

Before we could leave, Stuart and I had to find a place to stash the film's cold-blooded costar, a twenty-three-foot, 175-pound African rock python whom we affectionately called Loch Ness. His cage wasn't ready yet, but the bag he was in looked quite worn.

So . . . we decided to put him in my bathroom. We cleared everything out: we got rid of the towels, emptied the cabinet, locked the windows, and took up the small rug. Then we slid "Nessie's" bag in, undid the rope holding it closed, and left. I shut the door and put a sign saying "Hatari" ("danger") on it. Then I put another sign on the front door saying "DO NOT ENTER."

With everything looking safe, we took off.

Our trip to Nanyuki was a series of slips, slides, and spins down a road that, due to the kind of soil in that area, was as slick as oil from all the rain. Every few minutes, even at a speed of only five miles an hour, we ended up in a ditch. If the four-wheel drive couldn't get us out, we all had to push. (Our trip *was* successful, in that we weren't killed along the way!)

As we arrived back at the club, we noticed that a lot of people were hurrying toward the front apartments overlooking the pool. We parked our vehicle and headed in that direction.

Looking across the spacious lawn, I saw a crowd gathering around the door to my apartment. I raced ahead.

Upon reaching the door, I pushed the people aside to find that a flood of water was pouring out from under the door. One of the men told me that my room boy had gone in to clean and had found everything flooding. Seeing that the water was coming from the bathroom, he had opened the door, seen the giant snake, screamed, and raced away. Someone in the crowd said that he had been seen running in the direction of his village—about five miles distant. It was then that I noticed the "Hatari" sign lying on the grass some twenty feet away. Apparently, it had fallen off and was swept away by the water.

Stuart and I eased ourselves in. The apartment was a shambles. Everything that had been on the floor was now floating around the room. There was no sign of Nessie. Thank goodness that the boy had had the sense to close the door behind him!

I slowly cracked open the bathroom door, checking carefully to be sure the snake wasn't close enough to strike. This was not a reptile like those found in zoos and used to captivity. This was a tough, mean, "I-hate-humans" snake. If he ever got the chance to sink those teeth into somebody, constriction would start, and the victim would have a very tough time getting out from under those coils.

Nessie was lying over the sink. In crawling behind the faucets, he had turned them on.

I heard a familiar voice behind me.

"What happened here?" It was Bill. Although we were good friends, because the damage was so extensive, I didn't know how he would take it.

"Well, Bill, it's like this." I proceeded to tell him the story. His face lit up. A small chuckle turned into a roaring laugh. We all stood there, ankle-deep in the water, laughing our heads off at the predicament. That's what was so special about Bill—his good nature (at least when he saw that something wasn't intentional).

Then we got down to business. With Bill's help, we found about ten Africans who, with big smiles on their faces, swore they would help us. No, they wouldn't be scared. Yes, they would accept the extra shillings in their payroll.

I arranged for a large, strong, coffinlike box to be placed outside on the lawn. My plan was to take a large towel, put it on a long stick, and carefully open the bathroom door. Reaching in with the stick, I would drop the towel over Nessie's head so he couldn't see me. Then, at the right moment, I'd jump in and grab him by the neck. Stuart and a bunch of the guys would grab the coils, and together we would haul the snake out to the box. All the necessary Swahili was spoken to make sure that everyone understood his part in the effort. Then we all went into my apartment.

When I opened the bathroom door, Loch Ness was lying across the sink and down the floor, and half of him was in the bathtub.

Just as he moved in my direction, I dropped the towel over his head and placed both hands around his neck. Stuart, right behind me, grabbed some huge coils. Bill grabbed another five feet of snake. Of the ten men who had come to help, six screamed some profanities in Swahili and ran for the front door, all scrambling to get out at the same time. The remaining four each took a deep breath and hefted some coils. Then we all marched outside.

The snake pulled us this way and that, squeezing and sliding in an attempt to evade his captors. Somebody opened the lid of the box, and we dumped Nessie snake into it. One little guy couldn't get loose and ended up in the box while others were trying to close the lid. He was pulled to safety, and I then let go of the snake's head and slammed the lid shut. Then we all sat on the box, and drinks were passed around.

Later, a dozen men or so picked up the box to move it onto a truck, and the bottom fell out! I have never seen men run so fast, yet travel so little. But that's another story!

After the incident with Nessie, Bill gave me a charter membership in the club. He said that my frequent visits would guarantee more exciting animal adventures at the club than could be found on the veldt.

✳

One of the more exciting locations I've ever been to was the Caribbean island of St. Croix, in the Virgin Islands. The production was a remake of *The Island of Doctor Moreau* and starred Burt Lancaster, Michael York, and Barbara Carrera. It was our job to bring fifty-five highly trained exotic animals to a remote site on the island.

The animals were first flown to Miami, where they were transferred to a freighter to be taken to the location by sea. It was a regular Noah's ark, including lions, tigers, black leopards, and hyenas.

According to the film's story, the mad Dr. Moreau was injecting wild animals with a secret serum in the hopes of turning them into human beings. Moreau had created "lionmen," "tigermen," "pigmen," "buffalomen," and a dozen others. These roles were played by my trainers, who doubled as stuntmen. On many days there wasn't enough time after filming for them to change their clothes or remove their makeup before taking care of the animals. It was quite eerie to see a "wolfman" walking a tiger down the beach, or a "lionman" exercising a bear!

Watching Burt Lancaster perform was to watch a consummate actor, one who immersed himself so completely in the role he was playing that the world of external reality would seem to vanish. After a scene had been shot, a different Burt would emerge— warm and intellectually stimulating. Our working relationship developed into friendship in the months that followed, and he and his girlfriend Jackie later accompanied my family and me on safari to Kenya.

What stands out most in my mind about this particular film was the ending, which I assisted in developing. According to the story, the animal-men rebel against their mad creator, killing him, burning down his lab and house, and setting loose all the wild animals he had imprisoned as future victims in his insane scheme.

As part of the mayhem we created, a tiger attacked a "pigman" in the fiery lab; a leopard crashed through a glass skylight; a Brahma bull exploded through the wall of a burning building; and a black leopard attacked a man on the second-story balcony, with both then plunging to the ground below.

During the entire filming, there was not one scratch on either man or beast.

✳

Over the years, my various ranches have served as locations for scores of feature films, television series, and commercials. In addition to "Daktari," "Gentle Ben," and "Cowboy in Africa," segments of the "Lassie" and "Star Trek" television shows were often shot on our grounds.

The filming brought a lot of Hollywood stars to our ranches, including such people as Marlon Brando, Paul Newman, Betty White, Allen Ludden, William Shatner, Bo and John Derek, Sonny and Cher, and Carol Burnett.

Having known Carol since she was a teenager, I have always thought of her as a sister. One time, she and her kids came out to the ranch for a picnic—which we took via elephant!

Betty White and her late husband, Allen Ludden, were also close friends of mine. I had met Betty early in her career. Betty is a true animal lover. At one point, she and Ludden created a series called "Pet Set," for which I served as an animal behaviorist. I would bring unusual animals on the show—from three-ton elephants to fifteen-foot pythons. We'd share interesting animal facts with the audience, and Betty would take an active part in handling the animals on stage. Betty is one of those few people on earth who was born with a happy "aura" around her. If I were ever to choose a caretaker for the animals on this earth, Betty would be my first choice.

Another celebrity who frequented the ranch was the beautiful actress Debra Paget. A passionate animal lover, Debra owned a few exotic animals of her own, including a chimpanzee named Lord Murphy. She and Lord Murphy were quite a sight, pulling up to the ranch in their chauffeur-driven, gem-encrusted, white Cadillac convertible.

One blistering August afternoon, I was feeding the livestock, when I heard a male voice with a Southern accent ask me, "Can I give you a hand?"

"Sure!" I yelled over my shoulder, without turning around. "If you don't mind, give those pygmy goats and sheep a couple of flakes."

After I'd finished my afternoon chores, I went over to thank the stranger for his help.

"My name's Ralph—Ralph Helfer," I said.

He offered his hand. "Mine's Elvis. Elvis Presley."

Unbeknownst to me, Debra had brought Elvis out to the ranch with her and had dropped him off by the camel section while she went into the house to change into some ranch clothes.

I walked with Elvis over to the nursery, where Debra joined us. We sat on the floor and played with a couple of baby tigers and lions. Elvis had a natural ease around the animals, which was reflected in their obvious affection toward him.

This was the first of many such visits from Debra and Elvis, and not the last one in which he helped me with chores around the ranch.

✳

Many movie stars are fascinated with the idea of keeping exotic pets. When these animals get too large to be handled, their owners are compelled to give them up, usually to zoos. Some stars, however, have the foresight to see the danger that their pets can cause and try to place them in proper facilities before it's too late.

Such were the circumstances facing one Hollywood legend. . . .

I had just left the market, and my arms were full of groceries. As I cut across the parking lot, I noticed that a shiny black limousine with tinted windows was blocking my car. After putting my bags in the trunk, I walked over to ask the chauffeur to move so I could get out. As I approached, I saw a flash of what appeared to be an extremely hairy arm disappear behind the driver into the backseat.

"Excuse me, would you mind pulling back a bit so I can get out?" I asked. I tried to peek over his shoulder to see what the hairy thing might have been.

"Wait, Charlie," said a woman's voice. The back window was lowered partway, and the same muscular arm appeared through it. The woman's voice said, "Aren't you the man who has all those exotic animals on television?"

"Yes—I'm Ralph Helfer," I said.

The black hairy hand was stretching out, trying to touch me.

I knew by now that it belonged to a rather young chimpanzee. The window was lowered all the way. Inside, sitting on the plush interior, was a rather plump, attractive woman in her fifties, holding the leash of the chimpanzee. I recognized her immediately.

She smiled. "His name's Coffee. He has a cup every morning, and he'll shake hands with you if you want him to." I rarely touch other people's animals, especially chimps, as I know how cunning they can be. One minute they can be sweet and amiable, and the next minute a pair of fangs can be sunk into your flesh. However, this one seemed gentle and calm. I extended my hand; he did the same. Sure enough, my hand was indeed shaken, with a good deal of vigor.

"Hi, Coffee," I said. He looked at me with an inquisitive half-smile. His face was classic: he had large bright eyes that showed intelligence, ears properly centered on his head, a wide mouth, and a very strong jawline. His body was muscular and his hair was black, glossy, and well kept. He jumped up on the window ledge and, holding out both arms, began to whimper.

"He wants me to hold him," I told the woman.

"Well . . . normally, I wouldn't let anybody—but since it's you, go ahead."

Coffee leaped into my arms, hugging me and nuzzling my neck. I took the leash from the woman so it wouldn't pull on him.

"I've never seen him take to anyone like that!" she said.

Coffee started to go after the grocery bags of a woman who was walking by us.

"No, Coffee!" I said, pulling back sharply on his leash.

He looked at me as if to say, "Who the hell are *you* to tell me no?" but then he accepted my authority. He settled in my arms again.

"Sorry," I said to Coffee's owner, "but you know, it's not good to allow him to be undisciplined."

"How would you like to come to dinner at my home in Malibu?" she asked. "You and Coffee could get to know each other much better."

Chimps, with all of their cockiness, were one of my favorite animals, and I always jumped at the chance to work with them.

"I'd love to come," I said, passing Coffee back to her. He settled back into the plush seat and began making the electric window on his side go up and down.

The woman jotted something down on a piece of paper, which she then handed to me.

"Friday night at eight o'clock?"

"Yes, that would be fine."

She tapped on the glass partition, and the limousine started up. As it drove away, I studied the distinctive signature written above her address. The name written there was "Mae West."

On Friday, I drove out to Malibu. Miss West's elegant home was situated right on the beach. I was ushered into the luxurious living room, which was in semidarkness due to the heavy gold drapes hanging at the far end. The butler pushed a button and the drapes parted, revealing an absolutely breathtaking view of the Pacific.

Mae's sister, some other guests, and I were later sitting in the living room, chatting about various films being made in Hollywood, when our attention was drawn to the top of the staircase. There was Mae, posed in a gorgeous, white-brocade evening gown. She seemed to hesitate for a moment, and then, as though a director had yelled, "Action!" she slowly descended the curved staircase to the living room. Even though she was a rather small woman, she had a remarkable presence. In one corner of the room was a raised dais, on top of which was an elegant chair. This was Mae's chair. From it, she could gaze down and chat with her guests.

The house was full of paintings, and carvings of naked men. A large painting of Olympic athletes in the nude graced the second-floor landing, which one reached by a stairway whose railing featured carvings of key parts of the male anatomy. The hand of anyone ascending the staircase would naturally trail along these protruding parts.

In the months that followed, I became a frequent visitor at Mae's residence. Sometimes I went out to her ranch in the San

Fernando Valley, a beautiful spread that had its own racetrack! I also spent many hours playing with Coffee and teaching him new behaviors. As time went on, he and I became good friends.

Although he was one of the most beautiful and intelligent chimps that I had ever seen, he had been totally spoiled—and a spoiled chimp has the potential of being very dangerous. I had noticed from the start that if he couldn't have his way, he would grab your finger, put it in his mouth and hold it firmly with his teeth, then just look at you, as if to say, "Do I get my way, or do I bite?" I had a lot of training to do. The spoiledness gradually disappeared—at least, when *I* was around—and the new behaviors that I had added to his repertoire were greatly appreciated by Mae.

Meanwhile, young Coffee was growing rapidly and was as much of a handful as a rambunctious five-year-old boy—hardly a fit companion for a *grande dame.*

About four months after I'd first met Mae, she called me late one evening. "Hello, Ralph, dear? I want you to know that I've just made a very difficult decision. I've . . . decided to find a new home for Coffee. He's just getting too big for us to handle, you see? We love him so much . . ." the tearful voice broke, "and we feel you're the only one who could take good care of him the way we would. That is, *if* you'd like to have him."

"Of course I would, Mae," I hastened to reply reassuringly. "I know what it means to you to let him go, but I'll bring him over to see you often. He'll still be part of 'the family.' " I knew the pain she was going through; she had raised him since he'd been a baby. But now that Coffee was getting bigger, the only choice was to give him to a zoo or to someone who would care for him and love him in the way that she had.

There was another factor that weighed in favor of her offering Coffee to me. Mae knew that with me, Coffee could have a career in the motion-picture world, just like his "Mom."

There were tears all around when I left Mae's house with Coffee and headed back to my ranch. Mae had given me lists of his vitamins and minerals and of his likes and dislikes (which I knew already!); an elaborate wardrobe, which consisted of jackets, pants, suits, a hat, socks, and diapers; and a case of his favorite coffee!

Coffee took to his new surroundings immediately. Since he had become so well behaved, I kept him off the leash and with me as I attended to the ranch chores. Early each morning found him patiently waiting at the breakfast table for his "fix," a large cup of naturally decaffeinated coffee. He would add his own sugar—two teaspoons—and milk, and stir it all up. Then, with his regular diet of cereal and fruit, he would sit back and casually enjoy his morning breakfast. He was taught all the proper table manners, and he assisted in cleaning up after each meal.

Sometimes, however, Coffee could be a bit naughty.

I remember once when Elvis Presley came out to the ranch unexpectedly. Coffee was out, running loose, chasing the chickens and giving into his normal tendency toward mischief. I didn't hear the gate open and shut, but apparently he did.

Suddenly, I heard a sound that was something like "WHOOOFFF!" Walking round the corner, I saw Elvis flat on the ground, with Coffee jumping up and down on his chest. Coffee had apparently climbed up on the roof of the house and given Elvis a surprise greeting by launching himself down at him! I helped Elvis up, apologizing for Coffee's bad manners, but Elvis didn't seem to care in the least. Coffee, seeming to realize that his greeting had been a bit much, was busy brushing the dust off Elvis's pants.

Mae and her friends came out quite often to the ranch to see Coffee. While we picnicked on the front lawn, I would put Coffee through his new behaviors, such as opening combination locks, tying his own shoelaces, and using a can opener. As the years went by, he mastered a great amount of knowledge, and could always be counted on to perform—provided of course, that he'd had his morning cup of coffee first!

17

GENTLE IS THE WILD

I awoke to lightning illuminating my room. An electrical storm was raging over East Africa that seemed equal to the intensity of Noah's flood. But it wasn't the thunder that woke me; it was the distant roar of a lion. Zamba was afraid. Lightning always did scare him half to death, and I knew as I crawled out of bed that I would have to spend the night holding his paw to comfort him.

By the time I had walked the 300 yards to the animal compound, I was completely drenched. The other animals were all bedded down in their warm straw, under the thatched roofs. But not Zamba. He was pacing back and forth outside along the fence, all the while growling his displeasure. The torrential rain had soaked his large mane so that it hung down in a wet chunk, across his face and down his shoulder and back. Not so regal!

Another flash of lightning lit the compound for an instant, giving Zamba enough time to see me. I unlocked the door and went inside, talking "baby-talk" to him, in the way he liked.

"Hi, Zam, baby!" I immediately braced myself against the fence to help support the weight of his affections as he jumped on me. Then came the kisses, as Zamba's huge mass of a tongue tried to find my face between my hat and jacket.

I finally calmed him down enough to fasten a chain around his soaked neck. Off I went in the middle of the night, with a cowardly African lion, wondering what I should do next.

Zamba decided for me. A flash of lightning sent him bolting down the muddy road, dragging me on my derriere behind him. I saw a huge shape taking form before us and prayed it wasn't a rock. A door flew open, and the next thing I knew, we were inside the hut where the hay was stored. Puffing hard from his ordeal, Zamba plopped down on some straw.

Feeling revived, he attempted another kiss, which I quickly aborted. The next best thing was for him to lie with his massive bulk across me, which, of course, rendered me totally helpless. It was in this position that we both fell asleep, content that both the rain and the lightning would stay outside.

I awoke with the pungent odor of wet lion all around me. I could hear Zamba's heavy, rhythmic breathing. There was an occasional breath that seemed to be held forever and that was finally released with a heavy sigh. His massive paw was entirely wrapped around my waist, and with his every breath I could feel his dewclaw rub lightly against my skin. His mane, tickling my face, had awakened me—not hard to understand, as I was half-buried in it! So as not to disturb him, I gently eased myself up, which brought us face to face. His golden mane was definitely much thicker and softer here.

A small bright beam of African sunlight eased itself into our chamber, gleaming against the back of his ear. I could see all the veins, which reminded me of a freeway with no traffic. Every time Zamba exhaled, the light would slip off his ear and just graze the tip of one of his fangs, which protruded slightly from his lip. His exhaling also brought halitosis, which I'm sure lions must have invented. It was bad! I fought to enjoy watching Zamba's illuminated ear, but his breath won out. As I turned, the light started to fill the room. It was sunup.

With a straw, I gently tickled the inside of his nose. His eyelids moved. Again I tickled. The great nostril quivered and trembled, and finally he sneezed. I choked back a giggle! After he had settled down, I began tickling his nose again, but I failed to see the great amber eye that had blinked open and was watching me. I continued to drag the straw on the outside of his nose, until I came into direct contact with his huge, staring eyeball. Startled, I jumped! He jumped!

Then, rising up out of his warm comfortable bed, breath steaming in the chilly air, Zamba pounced! I dived under a huge pile of straw. He ran around in circles, digging and searching for me. If I hadn't laughed, he never would have found me. But the next thing I knew, he pounced on me, grabbing me in his paws like a mouse. Then, having won his victory, he began to lick my cheek with his powerful, sandpaper tongue. Knowing that it takes only a few licks to draw blood, I eased the licking by putting my arm in place of my cheek. Then, inching out from under him, I dusted myself off and pulled some straw from his mane. Then we went out into the crisp morning air, heading for the house.

Once we were in the house, Zamba settled by the fireplace, knowing that one of the first things I would do would be to light a fire. After doing so, I put on some coffee and headed for the bathroom to wash up. In the mirror, I noticed some long curved scratches on my back—no doubt some of Zamba's "marks of security" that I'd acquired during the storm!

After breakfast, Zamba got his usual brushing—a pleasure that he and I enjoyed equally. Zamba had an exceptionally large and beautiful mane. Its thick, coarse hair started at the top of his head and continued two-thirds of the way down his back. It then went across his belly and forward, getting thicker by the inch, until it spilled over his neck in a great shower of red-gold. He loved to be combed, but not too gently, or it tickled.

I gave Zamba's mane a quick, final brush and clipped on his chain leash (which we both hated), and we headed outside.

We were in Kenya filming *The Lion*. Ever since I'd been a kid, my greatest desire had been to go to Africa. And now, finally, I was here. It was not by luck or fate, but because Zamba had been raised with affection training.

Sam Engel, the producer of the film *The Lion*, had put out a call around the world for a full-grown lion to star in the film. The animal would have to be able to work safely with a child actress. No lion had been found that could fill the bill. The studio, Twentieth Century–Fox, was in the process of constructing a mechanical lion when I drove up to the gates with Zamba in the back of my station wagon. We walked into the main building and asked the receptionist where Mr. Engel's office was. The poor girl could only point up. Since it was only a two-story building, I felt that Zamba and I could handle the rest.

We were the only ones in the elevator, and the door opened

directly into Mr. Engel's office. The secretary there shrieked and proceeded to jump to the highest spot in the office—her desk. Mr. Engel, hearing the disturbance, came out of his office. He took one look, and—well, the rest is history!

Upon our arrival, we had been greeted with a Land Rover for hauling Zamba back and forth from base camp to the location. A well-known Nairobi artist had painted Zam's portrait on the doors.

Within two weeks, practically everybody in Kenya knew about us. Wherever we went, hordes of people would gather to see "the lion movie star." One day, we had taken off work early, and on the way home we decided to stop for a soft drink at a small town. The weather had been unbearably hot, and we figured we could also get a bucket of water for Zamba.

When we arrived at the local *duka* (shop), word spread quickly that Zamba was in the area. Just as we were pulling away, a crowd of people descended on the vehicle with such force that Zamba became nervous. Local African tribesmen, women, and children were screaming and yelling, and waving spears and shields. Zamba panicked and let out a huge roar, which caused the entire crowd to stampede away. We quickly took the opportunity to make a getaway ourselves. (Zamba never forgot that moment. From then on, whenever he saw a black African, he would snarl—not out of dislike, but out of fear. This was later to cause me a bit of concern.)

We then headed for the outskirts of the small village of Nanyuki. It wasn't long before Zam's breath had steamed up the inside of the windows. I opened the air vents and, as the windows cleared, Zamba's great head appeared through the vapor on the back window, startling a couple of Kikuyu women walking along the road.

It began to sprinkle, so I turned on the windshield wipers. This startled Zamba, and his whiplike tail smacked me square on the head! I shut off the wipers, but then I couldn't see the road, so I turned them back on and resigned myself to dodging Zam's tail all the way to the location site.

Putting the vehicle into four-wheel drive, I turned off the

Nanyuki tarmac and drove into a rough, desolate area called Rumaruti. Deep crevices, rocks, and raging streams all helped to make the ride an uncomfortable, bumpy trip. About every quarter mile, a wheel would fall into a rut or hit some obstacle, and Zamba's head would hit the ceiling.

When the rain stopped I opened the sunroof. Zamba raised himself up through the opening and rested his front paws on the roof of the car. With his huge head, massive chest, and mane sticking well above the opening, he rode like a monarch touring his kingdom. Making slow progress, we passed a small group of Masai walking tall, all decked out in their brightly colored garments, skin dyed ocher, and each carrying a spear. I waved. They waved back, then froze at the sight of Zamba, who let out a gutteral growl. In total confusion, they panicked. With all of Africa to run into, they chose each other's paths, and bumped into each other before finally taking off. With his ears perked forward, Zamba watched them disappear from sight.

At last, we arrived at the set. As I pulled through the gate, I was saluted by Njoke, the security guard. He was barefoot and was dressed in khaki shorts and a brown short-sleeve shirt with epaulets, and he was carrying a spear. "*Jambo, Bwana Simba!*" he said, with a broad grin.

I headed for the area where the picture was being filmed. After checking with the assistant director, I unloaded Zamba and put him in a specially built enclosure. The sun had come out, and the grass and shrubs were drying off. Feeling great, Zamba took off, leaping around in his new enclosure, occasionally slipping on the morning dew and falling on his face. In this cold, crisp morning air he would certainly give a great performance on film.

There was a lot of quiet excitement on the set. Although everyone was looking forward to the fight, all were aware of the danger involved. There are some people who wrestle "young adult" lions, but few who take on the big 500-pounders. Apart from the obvious reasons, the young adults still have a cub's playing instincts and thus love to "play" attack. But a mature lion's playing can easily revert to the instinct to kill.

Zamba would have to fight me controlled by *love,* by our

affection for each other. When he raced at me and launched into full attack, his years of training would tell him to pull his punches. When the massive paw slapped me across the face, or when my arm was between his fangs, the quiet words I would utter in his ear would guide him, and my hand on his mane would direct him.

It was now time for makeup. I had to double as a Masai warrior, so I stripped to a G-string and was submerged in a bathtub of Gentian violet and other long-sustaining dyes to color me totally black. I already had a deep tan from months in the African sun, so the dye had an unusual color affect, giving my skin the look of mahogany. Regular makeup had been tried at first, but it didn't work—the rain used in the scene washed it off. After trying several dyes, we came up with one that *really* stayed on. In fact, the color did not wash off for six months!!

Next came the Masai hairpiece, then the brilliant red wrap of cloth, and finally the spear and the knife. The only giveaway was the color of my eyes—bright blue. Otherwise, I was a full Masai warrior, but one who'd been born and raised in Chicago!

Would Zamba know who it was under the makeup and wardrobe, or would he think I was someone else? Would the color drive him to attack by visual association with his frightening experience in the Land Rover? I felt a shiver of fear.

The fenced-in encounter area was beautiful—high on the top of a mountain, surrounded by copper-colored rock, above a lush green valley speckled with acacia trees. This was to be the climax of the film. It was the story of a young girl, a Masai warrior, and a full-grown lion named King. The warrior falls in love with the girl, who has the lion as her pet. The lion's love for her is so strong that the warrior and the lion are forced to do battle over the girl's love. In the heat of the battle, the girl's father arrives. Amidst the screams of the girl, the father must shoot the lion to save the warrior's life.

The director's voice shattered my thoughts. "Attention, everybody! What we are about to do is extremely dangerous, not for us, but for Ralph. I must ask for absolute quiet." Because 80 percent of the people in the compound were African, his words were repeated in Swahili.

I picked up my spear and knife and entered the fenced-in area. Earlier, I had placed Zamba in the enclosure so he could get accustomed to the terrain. He had climbed to a high point on one of the cliffs, and as he looked over the valley below, it seemed for a moment that all time stood still.

With his full mane whipped by the wind and his head held high, his nose sniffing an Africa he had never known, Zamba seemed to be remembering. The wind was surely carrying a message. His past, his tradition, his great strength had always kept him a "survivor of the fittest." All of that had been exchanged for love, tenderness, and compassion. Is it right for as powerful an earth-god as he to be gentle? Could he live in a gentle jungle?

I turned away from the great creature and told the director we were ready.

"Okay, quiet on the set!" he shouted. "Roll camera, and . . . *action!*"

I gave Zamba the cue to attack. He turned and looked at me. My God, that look! At that moment, it seemed as though all the lions that had ever lived were peering through his eyes. Then he came! The cameras were rolling, and the girl was screaming her lines—"No, father! Don't shoot! Please father, don't kill him! Don't kill King!!"

What was that look in Zamba's eyes? What did I detect? In that moment, did he see into the past and revert back to his instinctive primitive ways? Or was it that he was seeing an African tribesman, not me? Never had he come on so strongly, with such determination. I poised for the spring. He sprang—five hundred pounds of feline power! Six times the strength of a man.

He hit me like a ton of rocks, and his great front legs and paws gathered me up like a toy. His mane choked my breath. For a split second I was allowed to roll out from under him, but he attacked again and again, until his great weight held me to the ground. His eyes narrowed, and his mouth opened. Four inches of fangs appeared.

I threw my arm out to protect my face. The fangs locked around it instantly, and held—softly. Yes, softly.

And then I knew. Even amidst the girl's screaming, the father's yelling, the gunshot, and the excitement of the moment, I knew what I had seen. The look in Zamba's eyes had been love. Our great love for each other was stronger than tradition, stronger than instinct itself.

Then the father shot the rifle, and Zamba was "fatally wounded." The squibs that I had placed under his mane earlier broke, and the "blood" ran down his mane.

Screaming and crying, "King! King!" the girl hugged and caressed the lion. His great head fell into her lap, and he "died."

The cameras stopped rolling. There was a moment of silence, and then pandemonium broke out. Amid applause, laughter, and cries of "Bravo!" I got up and walked over to Zamba. As I looked down at his still and "bloody" form, sheer terror shot through me at the horrible thought of his *really* being taken from me. I bent down over him. One great amber eye opened, and a forepaw shot up and caught me around the neck. He pulled me to him, and with his big, raspy tongue, he began licking my face.

We got up and walked out of the compound, out of the cheering and applause that comprised my world—and into his.

18

CLARENCE AND
JUDY

Clarence the lion was born cross-eyed. It was apparent as soon as his eyes opened. He was good-looking in all other respects—he had a large frame, and a regal head on his shoulders—and he was intelligent, but he was very, very cross-eyed.

We didn't notice that it caused him any particular vision problems, until one day when we were teaching him how to load into the back of a station wagon. The rear door was down, and one of our trainers got in and called to Clarence. As Clarence approached the car, the trainer enticed him with a piece of meat. He eagerly ran toward the wagon, jumped up, and ran smack into the side-door frame. He fell back, a bit dizzy from his encounter, then tried again. Again he clobbered his head on the framework. Getting up from the second try, he grumbled something nasty and gave me a dirty look, as though it had been my fault.

The next day our vet gave him the once-over. He said that animals, like humans, are sometimes born cross-eyed, but that generally one eye corrects for the other. Although this was an unusual situation, he felt that since Clarence was still quite young, the matter should right itself in time. To speed things along, he suggested a few things we could do to help Clarence in focusing.

We put Clarence on a special training program, setting up apparatuses that would teach him to use his eyes properly. One was a long, funnel-shaped walkway that corrected his direction by forcing him to focus as he moved along it. A similar device had a ditch dug on each side so that Clarence's feet would slip if he veered off the center path. This worked somewhat. Then an ophthalmologist came out to the ranch with a giant pair of prescription glasses that he swore would do the trick. Although Clarence did wear them (looking a bit silly), they proved to be of no use and were soon discarded. Looking back, I am sure the doctor was more interested in the notoriety than in helping Clarence.

As the years went by, Clarence seemed to outgrow his malady. Only occasionally was it noticeable. As for his overall appearance, well, only if you got down really close (and most people preferred not to) could you see the crossed eyes.

Clarence's animal costar was Judy the chimpanzee. I don't believe there was ever as unlikely a couple as these two natural enemies. Yet as star graduates of our affection-training program, they had developed a fond and playful attitude toward each other. Judy was a practical joker: she would pull Clarence's tail when he was sleeping or jump up and down on his back.

Judy became so proficient in acting that she could do a performance in one take. In fact, if the human actor needed too much rehearsal time, Judy would refuse to work. Only a short siesta or a cup of ice cream could convince her to return to the set.

When Judy was growing up, we allowed her to stay in our house from time to time and sleep in our bed. This was, for her and us, a nostalgic reminder of her babyhood. Her favorite spot in the bed was all the way down at the bottom.

Arriving home late one night with Judy, we had brought her home rather than walking her all the way back to the compound. She weighed about thirty-five pounds at that time, and she fit into a lot of Tana's old baby clothes—in this case, her pajamas.

Crawling under the blankets, she took her position down at the bottom of the bed and fell right to sleep. In the middle of the night, I awoke to a disruption in the bed. Judy was wiggling out from under the blankets. I knew she was trained not to leave the bed at night, so I lay still, watching her.

She managed to get out of bed and head down the hall. I was about ready to get up, when I saw the bathroom light go on! I waited. The door closed, and then I heard her piddling in the toilet. After some time, I heard the toilet paper being unrolled. I waited—more toilet paper. She always did use a lot!

The toilet flushed. I heard the water faucet turn on and off very quickly. Then, more toilet paper.

Then the light went out, and the door opened. I watched as Judy ambled back along the hall with the trap door of her pajama bottoms dragging behind her. She slid carefully into bed and was quickly back asleep. What training! I thought, before going back to sleep myself.

One day Judy caught a cold. The veterinarian attempted to give her a shot of vitamins, but without success—she would have none of it. Most chimps feel the same way about shots and have to be physically held down. In Judy's case, we decided to just forget about the shot; using restraint on an animal causes it to distrust its human cohort, and we would never violate the trust that Judy had in us.

After the vet left, Judy somehow got ahold of the syringe that he had tried to use on her and was soon playing with it, gently pricking her skin with the needle. I complimented her profusely, and I then decided to try an experiment. After getting from the vet a harmless spray that numbed the surface of the skin, I assigned one of my top primate trainers to Judy. We set up a program in which she would get a reward every time she pricked herself with the needle. It was no time at all before she understood what we wanted. Her desire to please, together with her insatiable curiosity and the lure of a reward, were enough to bring about the desired result: Judy gave herself a vitamin shot!

With such creative and intelligent stars as Clarence and Judy to work with, the writers on "Daktari" were continually coming up with unusual scripts. Once Clarence had to incubate a dozen abandoned ostrich eggs. Crazy premise! But it was cute when the chicks hatched and came crawling out all over him.

The most difficult thing that Judy was ever asked to do was to handle a snake. Chimps have a real fear of snakes and will go far out of their way to avoid them. However, after a calm and patient training program in which Judy was shown that the snake was harmless and posed no threat, she eventually held the reptile.

✳

Ivan Tors, one of the producers, and I were standing in the cage section one day, talking about "Daktari," one of our successful television series. We had been featuring Clarence in the show for some time, and the public's response was enormously favorable. The thought occurred to us to star him in his own movie, *Clarence the Cross-Eyed Lion.* But we could not do it unless we could find him a double, since the work load would be too much for just one animal.

We started to look high and low for another lion. He didn't have to be cross-eyed, just close to Clarence in overall appearance. Calls went out across the country, to individuals, zoos, and research institutes, but it was to no avail. The lions were too vicious to handle or train, or they were too young, too old, too short, and so on.

We did have one lion in our compound who looked *exactly* like Clarence. The only problem was that Leo would kill you if he was given half a chance.

Leo had been raised by a couple in Utah. When he'd started to kill the chickens around the ranch, the husband had beaten him for it. In reaction, Leo had bitten him severely. The man was about to have him put to sleep when we received a frantic call from the wife. She said that when the lion was young, they'd had him on a leash, and that he'd been "real good" until her husband had taken a stick to him. He had, she said, a "good heart." Would we rescue him? Feeling sorry for the cat, I agreed to take him.

Leo arrived mean, and he stayed mean. Anyone who went up to his cage was met by roars and snarls. But just because Leo was tough didn't mean we couldn't use him for film work. Under special conditions, he could be used to do "run-throughs" (meaning that he could run from point A to point B across camera) or to attack into the camera. Snarls were also in his repertoire, but he could never be put on a leash or be used in a scene that would require him to work closely with people. During the shooting of *Clarence,* we did use Leo—under tight security—whenever we needed a snarl. Clarence was just too good-natured to include snarls in his vocabulary.

One day, we were shooting a scene with Clarence, and everything was going quite well. When the time came for our lunch break, the trainers, unbeknownst to me, put Clarence in a nearby cage rather than back into his own, since they'd be using him again right after lunch.

During lunch, there was an animal emergency on the set across the valley, where we were shooting the series "Gentle Ben." The Clarence trainers were needed, and they headed off, saying that they'd be back in time for our next shoot.

We finished lunch, but no trainers appeared. I called the main office on my walkie-talkie to ask that Bob and Jose, two of my other top trainers, be sent down. Both were qualified to handle Clarence. When they arrived I told them to bring Clarence up, as we were nearly ready for him. A few moments later, Bob and Jose walked up with the lion.

"Where do you want him?" Bob asked.

"Just put him over there, and . . ." *Oh, my God,* I said to myself. *That's not Clarence.* Sweat broke out on my face. I looked around. There must have been sixty people standing nearby—crews, performers, ranch staff. I knew that the next thing I said could literally mean life or death.

I tried to act very nonchalant. "Okay, just put him over there. No, maybe there . . . !" I was losing it. I kept thinking that if the trainers realized they had Leo, they would handle him differently, and that this could trigger an attack.

I looked at Leo. Trying to stay cool, I said, "Tell you what, guys, take him back until we can set up a different angle." Bob looked annoyed. I was hoping that the lion wouldn't sense his attitude. They turned and headed back toward the cages.

I told everybody to take five, and I grabbed a small fire extinguisher from the side of a shed. We had used these very satisfactorily in emergencies before, since the blast will generally deter a lion from its prey. I quietly followed the trainers back to the cage. *How could they have mistaken the cage?* I wondered. The lion, yes—but the *cage?* Bob and Jose walked Leo into his cage and undid the chain—and then they stood there, *inside the cage, talking!* It seemed like an eternity. Then they walked out and closed the door. I dropped the fire extinguisher on the ground, hitting the handle by accident. However, nothing happened. It had been empty all the time! The trainers finally saw me and came over.

"What's up?"

I said nothing, but motioned for them to walk back to the cage with me. As we approached, Leo snarled and hit the cage with his full force, displaying his normal disposition.

Jose and Bob turned white. "You mean that was . . . ?"

"Yes, it *was!!* Why would you take him out? I don't understand."

The guys were shaking, and both had to sit down.

"When we came up," Jose said, "we just counted down the row to the one Clarence was in. He's always in number eight. *That's* number eight!!" He pointed to Leo.

We learned later that earlier that day, the cage on the end of the cat section had been removed to be used in an upcoming shot. This made Leo's cage number eight.

Leo looked on from his cage. Why, we asked each other, had he allowed the trainers to handle him? Many times, strange things happen during work with exotic animals. Maybe the men walking directly into the cage had taken him back to the days when he was a cub on a leash, being taken out for a walk, or maybe it just surprised him. I don't know. In any case, we never tried to put a leash on Leo again, and he never looked as though he wanted us to.

19

GENTLE BEN

One of our greatest accomplishments was "Gentle Ben," a series that ran for a number of years on national television. It was about a small boy and his family who lived in the Florida Everglades and who befriended a giant bear. The episodes, about courage, love, and adventure, stirred the hearts of millions, who tuned in each week to see what good deeds Ben would do this time.

Ben had come from Canada. Bears of the Great Northwest grow considerably larger than their Southern cousins. He stood well over eight feet tall and weighed 630 pounds. We got him when he was about two and a half years old—normally, too old to be trained. However, the people who had raised him were animal lovers who were never harsh or mean. Ben (whose name back then was "Bruno") had been fed, petted, and cared for like a child.

Pound for pound, bears are among the most powerful creatures on earth. I have seen them pull steel bars out of cages and turn four-by-four oak posts into splinters. Most bears have a short fuse and can become irritable at a moment's notice. But Ben, due to both his naturally mild temper and his gentle upbringing, was a perfect student for the affection-training program.

One of Ben's favorite pastimes was wrestling. We would take him out to a grassy area and tell him to sit, and then one of the trainers would slowly walk around him in circles. Ben would pretend he didn't know what was about to happen. Without warning, the trainer would make a dash for Ben. When he got within a few yards he would launch himself into the bear, wrap himself around the huge neck, and hang on! Ben would stand up to his full height, lifting the trainer off the ground. Then, reaching back with one massive paw, he'd scoop the trainer up and pull him around to the front.

Anybody wrestling Ben could do anything to him—pound, beat, pull, or pinch—it didn't matter! It was all good fun to Ben. He was too big to feel anything more than a tickle from most human beings.

Sometimes, an extra-large fellow would come along and ask if he could give it a try. Usually there was a very pretty girl with him to whom he most likely wanted to show off. "Sure," we'd say. "Go ahead—see if you can pin his shoulders to the ground!"

The big man would come at Ben like a tank, grabbing him around his midsection. Ben would then surprise the man by grabbing *him* and then flipping over and over, landing on top. He would then sit on his victim, looking for all the world as though he were terribly innocent. There was no way to get out from under Ben when he'd sat down on you! Teasing the man, we'd ask if he needed any help—an offer that was usually accepted. When we'd ask Ben to move his derriere, he'd look down as though he didn't even know the man was there, and then he'd let him up. We would always finish by giving some goodies to the man to feed to Ben.

One of Ben's best friends was Clint Howard, the actor who played the role of the small boy in the series (his parents were played by Dennis Weaver and Beth Brickell). Clint was just a small tyke, and Ben treated him as though he were a cub. He responded readily to the boy's wishes. When Clint asked him to come, sit, or stay, Ben complied quickly. One of Clint's favorite things to do was to put a piece of candy in his mouth and have Ben take it. Ben had an enormously long tongue, and Clint would bite down teasingly and not let him have the candy. Ben would proceed to lick the boy's entire face until Clint gave the candy up.

Most of "Gentle Ben" was shot in Florida during the hot, humid season, when it was difficult for everybody to work—and the bears were no exception. The swamp chiggers and other crawling life would burrow into their fur, causing them to itch. During breaks, Beth Brickell could be seen helping the trainers comb the chiggers out of Ben's fur, while he lay there in complete ecstasy.

We had three other bears who served as Ben's doubles, each one specializing in something. One was Ben's absolute physical double. It was hard even for us to tell them apart. However, this second bear didn't have Ben's disposition, and he was used only if we felt that Ben was being overworked. The second bear was used in run-throughs. So as not to tire out the real Ben (who didn't like to run much), we used the run-through bear.

One cage, with this bear in it, would be set behind the camera. The second cage could be set anywhere—over the hill, in a house, behind a ridge, wherever. When the director yelled "Action," the door of the bear cage would be opened. Out would run Ben II, who would race for the other cage. The trainer awaiting him would blast a horn so that the bear knew where he was. The bear also knew that upon his arrival he would be met with all of his favorite fruit. Not exactly "affection training," this was more on the "reward" system, but we found that for this particular animal it worked best. Over the hill and down the road, lickety-split, would come "old run-through," as we called him. Even when approaching the cage he would never slow down. The trainer would open the slide door. As the bear ran in, he would "throw on the brakes" before hitting the back of the cage. Then he would settle in for a nice meal of watermelon, oranges, apples, and other tasty morsels!

The third bear was our fighting bear. He would take on anything the script called for: bear versus dog, bear versus mountain lion, bear versus four men, anything. The writers could dream up any action for a fight bear, and Ben III was always ready. All the fight scenes were, of course, simulated. All the punches were pulled, and training was done well in advance.

Unlike his human costars, Ben often slept late. He would lie drowsily in his cage for hours, yawning, stretching, scratching, oblivious to the world around him. As the noise from the crew became louder and the scent of hot coffee and doughnuts wafted into the cage, Ben would roll over and head for the front of his cage so he could watch the activity going on—and perhaps beg for a doughnut or two. Sometimes his trainers would take him out for a walk, perhaps heading over to the stream for a good swim. On a lucky day they'd take him over to the cafeteria to do a "sit-up" for the cook, knowing he'd be given a treat for his efforts.

On this particular morning we were shooting a scene from the "Daktari" series on the ranch property. The location chosen for the first shot was adjacent to the bear section. This area was bordered on one side by a grove of trees, and on the other by train tracks, which were hardly ever used. Only an occasional freight train lumbered by.

The animals were unusually quiet. The big cats were sleeping late. Modoc, Margie, and the other elephants were munching lazily on some hay while their keepers washed down their sleeping quarters.

Just as the crew had finished setting up their first shot, we heard it. At first it sounded like an earthquake; then the low rumbling increased to an ominous, earth-shattering roar. A 100-ton locomotive was coming down the track at a high speed, far too fast to make the curve. It took only a few seconds. I looked around in time to see this monolithic steel giant come off the track, hesitate in midair, and then crash into an area close to the bear section. The body of a man was hurled through the air and came to rest farther down the track.

Steam was rising from the monster, and oil was spurting everywhere. Elephants broke their chains and ran. Camels and zebras bolted. The big cats hit their cages so hard that some actually moved the joints securing them to the cement pads. People were screaming and racing everywhere. I yelled to the production assistant to call for an ambulance, while a group of trainers ran to help the man on the track.

The area around the runaway engine was devastated. Trees, cages, and walkways all lay in a ground-up heap. I could make out the edges of Ben's cage under the engine. We were all in shock; it had happened so quickly. The engine had just missed the hyenas and two harp eagles, but it appeared that at least three twenty-foot-long cages had been buried under the locomotive.

There must have been fifty people gathered around the area. Someone yelled, "Ralph, look!"

Across the ranch, coming toward us, were the figures of two men and a bear. When the men saw the train on its side, they started to run. As they got closer and closer, I saw that the two men were Ben's trainers, and that the bear with them was *Ben!* They raced up the embankment. Ben was hugged and petted and cried over, and everybody was talking at once about how lucky we were that Ben's trainers had chosen this moment to take him out for a walk.

Two of the three train crewmen survived; the engineer had been killed while trying to stop the train. Amazingly, our only loss was the animal cages.

The fuss we made over Ben didn't faze him in the least. To him it was just another television or movie scene, not all that different from other scenes he'd done. But to us it was a minor miracle.

20

C. J.

The duckling, a little puff of warm, yellow-orange feathers, was only one day old. Somehow it had gotten separated from its mother and was now running helter-skelter around the garbage cans, in and out of fences and gopher holes.

"He's over here . . . well, he *was,* anyway," yelled a trainer.

"Now he's headed back your way," I yelled, as I fell over the garbage-can lids.

"I've got him cornered at the hay bales!" My daughter, Tana, was jumping back and forth, waving her arms, trying to keep the duck contained.

We formed a circle so that we could try to grab the puff before it disappeared into the cage of Lobo, our white Arctic wolf. Lobo, who was about five years old and weighed 150 pounds, was gentle enough to play with our dogs. However, wolves love duck—and even though for Lobo the baby duck would be little more than an hors d'oeuvre, it was truly a delicacy. Lobo had glimpsed the morsel and had been pacing back and forth whenever the duckling looked as though it were headed his way.

Picking up his little wings, the duckling headed straight as an arrow for Lobo's home. Tana and I gasped in unison. Lobo licked his chops in anticipation. We ran to head him off, arriving at the cage at the same time as the duckling. Before we could grab him, he'd whizzed by under our feet. Then he ran right under Lobo's face, across the cage, and out the other side! Lobo stood panting while we breathed a sigh of relief.

But our relief lasted only a second. The duckling was now

hurtling toward the primate section, which consisted of ten large cages and a dozen or so smaller ones that housed our collection of chimpanzees, gorillas, baboons, and various smaller monkeys.

Off we went again, in the direction of the small ball of yellow and orange, which seemed intent on its own extermination. We ran around the corner of our orangutan, C. J.'s, cage, and froze at what we saw.

C. J. was flat on his back, asleep, with one huge arm extending through the bars and out onto the ground. The duckling had stopped when it arrived at C. J.'s huge hand, which was perfectly still. The little bird stared at the great, hairy thing. Then, probably assuming that this was some kind of grassy knoll, it began to peck and hunt amongst the coarse red hair looking for food.

The duckling continued on its rounds, picking at the hand, until the orangutan's fingers flicked out in an attempt to brush the "fly" away. The movement scared the little bird half to death! As soon as the fingers relaxed, however, back came the duck. What he found there (probably some leftover bits of lunch) must have been really good!

C. J. was in his prime. He weighed around 275 pounds, most of which was in his huge belly! His fur was reddish-gold and quite thick. His small, beady eyes peered out from beneath a prominent brow. He had the strength of four men—four *big* men—and yet he could be extremely gentle. Since he was arboreal, his arms were long, and his hands were massive (each was more than double the length of a man's hand), so as to support his huge body as he swung from branch to branch, high above the ground! Standing up, he could easily touch an eight-foot-high ceiling. C. J. was magnificent!

Now I watched in horror as the duckling jumped suddenly into C. J.'s palm. Tana, afraid of what might happen next, had to turn away. However, the duckling's weight was so slight and C. J.'s palm so thick that I guess the big ape didn't feel a thing.

Now the duck was really at home, hunting and pecking and scratching contentedly as it went. For a moment, it got entangled in the three-inch-long, bronze, wavy hair on C. J.'s wrist. But then it quickly freed itself, and headed up the arm!

By now, C. J. was beginning to stir, and his hand sailed through the air to scratch a spot just inches away from the little duck. The giant opened his eyes. Tana stifled a scream. This was it! The duckling was moving toward C. J.'s head! Then, in one slow roll, the orangutan was on his belly, sending the duckling scrambling to keep from falling off or being smashed. C. J. rested his chin on the ground, and his eyes took in the small intruder that was happily heading his way. The duck crossed over C. J.'s elbow and biceps and jumped up on his shoulder. We figured that with one more move, it would be history. By now the baby duck was maneuvering like a logroller, as C. J. flipped over onto his back again. Once the ape had settled down, the duck jumped up on his head! Walking down the path between C. J.'s eyes, he headed straight for the mouth.

C. J.'s eyes followed every move the duck made. As it passed the nostrils it was startled by the hot breath, which blew him onto the ape's upper lip. C. J.'s huge, flexible lips twitched, creating what must have felt like an earthquake to the duckling. Then, putting his hand under his chin, C. J. sat up and let the duck fall right into his hand! He put his nose against the baby bird's body and sniffed. Reaching up with his other hand, he extended one finger—and began to stroke the duckling! We couldn't believe our eyes! It looked like Fay Wray with King Kong. C. J. was in love!

This experience began a long-lasting friendship between C. J. and the duckling. From then on, the duckling almost never ventured out of C. J.'s cage. He could generally be found pecking and scratching around on the ape's belly, or curled up asleep somewhere on the big, furry body. C. J. was always careful not to roll over and hurt his roommate.

*

In comparing the attitudes of gorilla, orangutan, chimpanzee, and human, I always put the gorilla and orangutan together, and the chimp with man. This is primarily because the first two are basically introverted, and the latter two are extroverted. The gorilla and orangutan seem to live a more tranquil existence, moving slowly, eating quietly, and rarely having family quarrels or distrusting their fellow apes. They are not nearly as mischievous as chimps or, for that matter, humans.

No animal related to other animals better than C. J. did. Had the duckling run into the chimp's cage, I believe he would have been devoured on the spot. C. J. was one of the good guys! He was a gentle animal, a lover of people, animals, and life in general. He rode horses, traveled in cars, and kissed the people he liked. However, if someone had ticked him off for some reason, he would ignore the person by turning his back.

C. J.'s outstanding talent and personality made him famous throughout the industry. Always in demand, he did a number of movies, television talk shows, cameo spots in TV series, and magic shows. C. J. was a star. He was to the animal world what Laurence Olivier was to the human.

One day I received a call from my old friend John Derek, asking if I would be interested in supplying all the animals for his upcoming movie *Tarzan, the Ape Man.* He would direct it, and his lovely wife, Bo, would star. I was eager for the chance, and C. J. and I, along with two trainers, met with John and Bo at MGM to discuss the filming.

Bo greeted C. J. with natural warmth and understanding. She knelt down a few feet away from him, a smile on her gorgeous face.

"Hi, C. J."

C. J. sat looking at the office, the people in the room, and, finally, Bo. He got up, ambled over to her, and sat down. She took her finger and traced it along his fingers, across his palm, and up his arm. C. J. watched, his eyes following her hand up to his shoulder. Then he reached over, picked up her hand, smelled it, and kissed it!

Bo ran her fingers through C. J.'s long red hair. He lay flat on his belly while she scratched his back. It was love at first sight. Bo and C. J. were an item. To see the petite figure of the blond-tressed Bo beside C. J.'s massiveness was breathtaking, the epitomy of "beauty and the beast." The natural way in which they cared for each other and the gentleness with which he handled her were awe-inspiring. Everyone seeing them together was captivated by the special love they showed each other.

The movie was to be shot in Sri Lanka, and the animals would have to be transported there by jet. This was not something new to our animals, most of whom had traveled extensively. We had several aluminum cages which were lightweight yet very strong. An average cage for a lion, adult orangutan, or bear was about six feet long, two and a half feet wide, and five feet high. Water was always available. If a flight was longer than five hours, food was given en route; otherwise, it was best to wait until reaching the destination. The trainer flew on the same plane and took care of things personally.

Many animals were to be used in the picture, but to me—and I am, of course, prejudiced—C. J. was the one who stole the show, with Bo. My favorite moment came at the end of the movie, during the credits, when film was shown of Bo and C. J. rolling around and playing together. No acting was needed. We could have been in Eden! They were heavenly.

Back in the states, Warner Studios was interested in having C. J. costar as Clint Eastwood's sidekick in the movie *Any Which Way You Can*. I met Clint at his office to talk about the film. He was anxious to be introduced to C. J.

From the beginning, the two hit it off. C. J. had an instant respect for Clint, probably due to the actor's size, and he treaded carefully until he got to know Clint better. Clint, for his part, would have made a great animal behaviorist had he not chosen to be an actor. His handling of C. J. was second nature—off-the-cuff and mellow. They would clearly be pals for life!

C. J.'s favorite human being was a young, good-looking, well-muscled, blonde "Adonis" named Jack. Jack was one of C. J.'s trainers, and he and the ape had a special relationship, one that went beyond that of trainer and animal. They were inseparable friends; they ate together, and they were always playing and wrestling. They'd snooze together on the grass or spray each other with the garden hose. They could sit for hours picking and preening each other.

C. J. would climb up Jack as though he were climbing a tree, and then would attempt to give the trainer a kiss. Jack would gently bite C. J.'s lips, holding them together with his teeth. This would make C. J. giggle, and the two would end up rolling around on the ground, tickling each other.

If C. J. got a scratch on his arm, he would go to Jack, who would examine it, pick it, clean it, and sometimes bandage it. And if Jack had a scratch and showed it to C. J., the same situation would occur in reverse! The orangutan would make a big to-do over the injury, mimicking Jack's behavior with bandages and iodine.

Sometimes, I had Jack bring C. J. up from the primate section to visit at the house in the evening. My doorbell would ring many times as C. J. pressed it over and over. C. J., always dressed for the occasion, would then take off his jacket, shake hands, hand his jacket to me, and immediately head for the kitchen. There he would open the refrigerator, get a Coke, some cheese, an apple or maybe a banana—whatever interested him. He'd load it all onto a plate, which he removed from the cupboard along with a handful of candy. He'd open a bag of popcorn, cradle it in his arm, and then head back to the living room, where he'd carefully lay everything out on the floor.

"His" cushion, made especially for him by the children at a local orphanage, was yanked off the sofa and added to the collection on the floor. Turning on the television, he would search to find the most exciting program. To him this was generally a Western, because he loved to watch the horses! Then he would lie back with his head on the pillow, surrounded by his goodies, totally in heaven as he tuned out for the next hour or so.

C. J. owned a complete wardrobe: short coats, pants, suits, tuxedos, hats, and shoes, all custom made. Some were very expensive, having been designed and tailored for his starring role in "Mr. Smith," a television series that I later produced at Paramount Studios.

The show was about an orangutan who, due to an accident, develops a high enough I.Q. to become a lawyer. Although C. J. could do everything the script required of him, there was one thing he couldn't manage. C. J. couldn't talk. Affection training does have its limits!

So, a special-effects team was hired to build a computer that sent remote-control commands to a mechanical model of C. J. made of wood, metal, and bolts. When it was completed, the model could open and close its eyes and move its lips and body. In addition to the computer activation, technicians worked *within* the puppet to make arm and body movements. The mouth was intricately wired to respond to the electrical board, through which the operator would move the lips and mouth by pulling and pushing the levers. After a few days, the operator had the puppet "talking." To find the right voice for C. J., we tried out many people, finally ending up with the voice of an executive at the studio.

It was a great day when the first show was aired. The "real" C. J. was used most of the time, and it was only when Mr. Smith had to talk that the model was used. However, being around C. J. and his computerized double could be confusing. The two together became interwound, as some folks began to believe that C. J. could actually talk! People would walk up to him and ask him questions, and they would look concerned or annoyed when he didn't answer. Finally, blushing with embarrassment, they would realize what they had done and walk away.

During the run of this production, C. J. became "one of the boys," getting up every morning at six o'clock with the rest of us. He would head for the bathroom, wash his face with soap, and dry off with a towel. He'd put a couple of squirts of under-arm deodorant on, occasionally missing and hitting the mirror. Later, the trainers would rub oils into his body to keep his skin soft and his hair in good condition. Then he would head off to wardrobe, putting on a tux, a suit and tie, or maybe jeans and a T-shirt, depending on which show he was working in.

Finally, we would hand him the leash to his "pet" poodle, Cheetah. Cheetah was a lovable white toy poodle, a member of one of several generations of poodles that had been born on the ranch (since, in addition to our exotic animals, we had many highly trained domestic animals).

Although C. J. and Cheetah lived on the same ranch, they had never really known each other until Cheetah met C. J. one day at the studio. She was interviewing for a dog-food commercial, and C. J. had just come from working on an episode of "Hill Street Blues." When Cheetah saw C. J. she broke away from her trainers, ran over to him, and, without hesitation, jumped up into his arms.

It is rare for an animal to respond to an animal of another species without showing some fear or, at least, caution. This was true romance! C. J. held the small poodle in his arms while being licked with kisses.

The two became inseparable. When the Paramount executives saw them together, they felt that C. J.'s character could have a pet. Why not? So, what was real in life became perfect for the series.

Major stars always want their own trailers, and C. J. was no exception. During mid-season, the studio bought a beautiful, custom-made trailer for him to live in while on location. C. J.'s trailer was deluxe even by human standards, with its living room, sleeping quarters, bathroom, and kitchen, in which we used to prepare his special diet. Reporters and photographers flocked into the trailer every day to do stories on his latest antics and achievements.

C. J. sat in on every script conference. All of his action, stunts, and dialogue were itemized and given to us several weeks before the shoot so we could teach him to "perform" to the best of his ability. His high intelligence allowed us to merely walk through a scene with him to familiarize him with everything required.

With a series of verbal commands, such as "Stop," "Stay," "Sit down," "Stand up," "Wave," "Pick it up," and so on, C. J. was able to do a complete scene. He simply had to watch us for his command. Sometimes his actions became so routine that he would perform without any help.

Since nobody was built the way he was or could do the things he could, C. J. did his own stunts. His huge chest, long, powerful arms, and huge feet allowed him to climb effortlessly, anywhere he pleased.

There are some people who object to the idea of an orang-utan—or any other animal—wearing human clothes, watching television, or starring in movies. These people feel that these things take away the animal's pride and dignity. And if animals were entirely safe in their natural habitats, I would agree. But things have changed, and today the only safe place for most animals seems to be with human beings who will protect them. Isn't it better to have animals as friends, letting them provide entertainment and education, than to have them succumb to a poacher's machete and end up on the wall as a trophy, or on someone's back as a coat?

Every day, the number of animal species moving toward extinction grows. Zoos try hard to preserve these species, and they are to be commended. However, zoological institutes do not believe in any system that "humanizes" animals. The many wild-life organizations worldwide send trained professionals, supplies, and money to the wilds and set up sanctuaries—and still animals die. Their deaths are caused by poachers, by the encroachment of towns and cities that are taking away their habitats and by farmers protecting their crops. The animals are losing the battle.

If we are to save endangered species—orangutans and gorillas among them—we need more than the efforts of a few thousand individuals with limited resources. We need a global commit-ment, supported by the world powers and backed by stiff penal-ties to punish those who would take the permanent destruction of our wildlife lightly or pursue it for sport or financial gain.

In the meantime, it is possible that such hands-on, nonintrusive techniques as affection training could be used in conjunction with other progressive programs to help ensure that these endangered species have a better chance of survival.

C. J. was one animal who would never be exposed to a poacher's rifle. True, he probably couldn't have cared less about the perks of his lifestyle—the fancy clothes, media attention, and devoted fans. But he did appreciate our companionship and the love he received from those close to him.

And, in spite of some people's belief to the contrary, C. J. actually didn't become more "humanized" by being with us, any more than a giraffe becomes "zebra-ized" by associating with zebras. If anything, C. J. made *us* more human by showing us love and affection, loyalty, and devotion.

C. J. was a teacher, a loyal friend, and a pal. My relationship with him—like the one I had with Zamba, my lion—epitomized that special something that happens to people who really allow animals into their hearts. Whatever you were before is only enhanced by having the animal enter your world, and vice versa.

I remember an occasion when I was lying on the floor with C. J., watching television. There was a bowl of popcorn on the other side of him, and every so often his huge hand would dip into the bowl, bringing out a rather large handful. Then, one by one, he would toss the popped kernels into his mouth and crunch away as he watched the screen. If someone walked in front of the TV or otherwise blocked his view, he would first try to look around the person. If this didn't work, a hand would reach up and gently nudge the offender aside.

One time, I wanted some popcorn, but for some reason I didn't ask C. J. to pass me the bowl (which he would have done, posthaste). Instead, I just started to watch him and not the TV. He didn't acknowledge my glare, but just kept stuffing his face with popcorn.

Then I saw his eyes shift in my direction—not his head, just his eyes. I said nothing. His eyes were now watching me out of the corner of his lids. The hand with the popcorn became slower and more indecisive.

I kept looking. The hand now rested on his belly, motionless. A few pieces of popcorn lay on the floor where he had let them dribble through his fingers.

I watched.

C. J.'s face turned a deep red. Finally, without moving his head, he reached over with his other hand, grabbed the bowl, swung it all the way over, and set it down beside me. Then he put his hand back in his lap. His eyes shot back and forth, anxiously.

He put his arm on the floor and then, crablike, scooted his fingers over to my hand. His head never moved. Bumping my fingers with his, he took my hand, placed it in the bowl of popcorn, and waited.

My hand was motionless.

Now his huge body stirred. He pivoted around and looked at me.

I looked back, stonefaced.

He leaned forward onto his elbow.

Then, reaching down, he picked up one piece of popcorn in his huge fingers, and like a giant hoist, carried it to my mouth. I opened it, and he proceeded to place the popcorn in my mouth. Just as his finger dropped into my mouth, I clamped down!

I have never seen 275 pounds of animal leave the ground with such speed! Holding his finger gently but firmly in my mouth, I maintained my grip. We both knew that he could pull his finger out anytime he chose. Throwing his full weight on my lap, he turned on his back, reached up, and started to tickle me with his free hand.

That did it! I let go of his finger, and we launched into a rough-and-tumble free-for-all that nearly knocked over the TV.

Afterward, we settled down to one of C. J.'s favorite shows, "Gunsmoke." As we lay there, I noticed that the bowl had again ended up on C. J.'s far side. He saw me looking, and, quick as a flash, he grabbed the bowl and put it between us!

C. J. never got bored. He had an uncanny way of finding things to keep himself amused. I remember once when I was relaxing in the animal compound, watching him. He had emptied his food bucket and was now placing small rocks in it. With his giant index finger he was picking up all the rocks he could find and putting them, one by one, into the bucket. Finally, it was full. Then, with his eyes squinting with amusement, C. J. picked up the bucket with both hands, held it over his head, and, with a flip of the wrist, turned it upside down. As the rocks came crashing down on his head, his body shook with giggles. Then he started the little game all over again.

We had trained C. J. from an early age to play with other exotics. It was not unusual to see him romping with two or three young tigers, lions, or bears.

For convenience and sanitation, we had taught C. J. to use the toilet, which he did whenever he needed to. Pulling the seat down, using toilet paper, and flushing were all handled with the delicacy of a well-raised human being. As with any curious child, there were times when C. J. would simply stand there, flushing and reflushing, watching the water fill up and go down again. We would have to call him a number of times before he would leave.

Riding in the truck, C. J. always liked to sit by the window, with his arm dangling over the side.

As we drove down the freeway, people would call to him, yelling "Clyde!"—his name in the movie *Any Which Way You Can*. In the film, C. J. had used a right-turn hand signal to knock the "heavies" off their motorcycles. Whenever he was in the truck he played to his audience, giving them his famous signal. Everybody would break up.

Sometimes, when he was dressed up in his sport outfit, complete with hat and scarf, he would sit with his arm on the armrest, gazing out the window with a certain look of wisdom on his face. Some animals develop this look as they mature. The adage that wisdom comes with age holds true for animals as well as people. The experience of living and of learning how to survive gives a certain, earned look of dignity to an animal.

C. J. often wore a pair of sunglasses, which added to his look of distinction. Many people in the vehicles passing by looked directly at him and never even realized he was an orangutan.

One evening when we were at a gas station, a man came over to the passenger side of the car and asked C. J. for directions! C. J. rolled down the window, reached out one long, hairy arm, grabbed the guy by the neck, pulled him in, and planted a big wet kiss on his lips. Fortunately, we had finished filling up. We were out of there FAST! Looking in the rearview mirror, I saw the guy still standing there in shock, map in hand. That's one kiss he'll never forget!

One day, after shooting for a "Mr. Smith" episode was over, C. J., a trainer, and I piled into our truck, like a bunch of guys going out on the town. We had decided to get some refreshments to take home.

At the 7-Eleven store, I rolled C. J.'s collar up as we went into the snack area, passing the cashier and four or five customers. C. J. chose some bubble gum, six candy bars, several handfuls of peanuts in packets, and one or two other favorite snacks. As a couple of Cokes were added to the collection, he put the overflow between his toes. The trainer and I got something for ourselves and headed for the counter to wait our turn. I gave C. J. twenty bucks as he stood in line behind me. When his turn came, he handed the money to the cashier, who rang it up and handed the change back to him. He calmly tucked it in his pocket, picked up his bag of supplies, and followed us out of the store. Not one person in that 7-Eleven appeared to notice that they had been shopping with an ape!

This scenario was played over and over again. Once, C. J. carried a baby chimp wearing a big diaper into the market. C. J. himself was wearing an oversized T-shirt, Levi's and jogging shoes and had a towel hanging around his neck. On his head, he wore a baseball hat, and of course he had on his ever-present shades. A woman approached, asked if she could see the baby, cooed over it happily, stroked its chin, and said, "How sweet!" But she made no comment about the "guy" *holding* the baby!

Months later, I was in Brazil for the shooting of my movie *Savage Harvest,* when I got the news that C. J. had died of a heart attack. I couldn't believe it. He had been big and healthy. I was stunned, as were his many friends around the world. The keepers said that just the day before they had seen him swinging and playing in his specially built cage, looking great; the next morning, he was gone.

People who knew C. J. will always remember him as a friend and ally, an animal who reached out to us humans to bridge the gap between us and bring us into his world. Those of us who were fortunate enough to enjoy his company know that with him, there truly was no gap to bridge. He had been one of us, and we had been one with him.

Rest well, old buddy!

21

THE FLOOD

It was raining that morning, as usual. For weeks it had been coming down—sometimes heavily, with thunder and lightning, and sometimes with just a mist of light rain. But it was always there, and by now the blankets, the beds, and the whole house were constantly damp.

My career was at a peak. I'd spent twelve years struggling to get to the top, and I had finally made it. My life was pretty good. I had just completed the back-to-back shooting of "Daktari" and "Gentle Ben," and I was living at our new ranch, Africa U.S.A., with 1500 wild animals and a crew of dedicated keepers and trainers.

The ranch was beautiful. Nestled at the bottom of Soledad Canyon, about thirty miles north of Los Angeles, the property snaked for a mile down the canyon beside the banks of the Santa Clarita stream. The highway wound above it on one side, the railroad track on the other.

We'd had heavy rains before, and even a few floods, but nothing we couldn't handle. There was a flood-control dam above us, fifteen miles up the canyon, and we weren't too worried about the stream's overflowing. But just to make sure, we had asked the city's flood-control office to advise us. They checked their records for the biggest flood in the office's hundred-year history, and calculated that to handle one that size we would need a channel 100 feet wide, 12 feet deep, and 1 mile long. It cost us $100,000 and three months of hard work, but we built it. It was worth it to feel safe.

Toni and I had grabbed a few hours' sleep before leaving the house, which was located off the ranch up on a hill, and heading out into the rain again early this morning to make sure our animals were dry and safe.

On arriving at the compound, Toni went over to check on the "wild string," a group of lions, tigers, bears, and leopards that had been donated to us by people who never should have had them in the first place. Hopeless animal lovers that we were, we had taken them in, even though we knew that very few spoiled mature animals could ever be indoctrinated with affection training.

I checked at the office for messages, then headed for "Beverly Hills," our nickname for the area where our movie-star animals lived—Gentle Ben, Clarence the cross-eyed lion, Judy the chimp, Bullfrog the "talking" buffalo, Modoc the elephant, and many others. The rain had become a steady downpour by the time I arrived there. Everything seemed to be in order, so I went on to the rhinos. No problems there, either.

As I left the rhinos, I noticed that I could no longer jump over the stream that ran beside their barn. I was starting to get a little concerned. The sky was now opening up with a vengeance. I wrapped my poncho around me and continued my tour of inspection.

I was wondering how Toni was making out with the wild string when Miguel, a Mexican keeper who had been with us for six years, arrived to care for the animals in the Beverly Hills section. He smiled his broad, gold-capped grin, then disappeared around a bend of the stream.

Then my head trainer, Frank Lamping, arrived. He told me that the earthen dam above us was about to go. To prevent the dam from bursting, the flood-control people were opening the floodgates to release the pressure. We were to watch out for some heavy water coming downstream.

The crew had all been working continuously from morning until night since the rains had begun, to make sure that the ranch was safe. Now we had to redouble our efforts.

I told Frank to check the stock area. A trainer yelled from the roadway above that he had the nursery section under control.

I found some pretty badly undermined cages in my area and set to work with a shovel to fill the erosion. I was looking down at my shovel, working hard, when I heard a noise. It was a low roar, and it was quickly becoming louder and closer. I remember just looking over my shoulder, and suddenly there it was—a wall of water carrying with it full-sized oak trees, sheds, branches. Down it came, crashing and exploding against the compound, uprooting cages, overturning buildings, trucks —anything in its way.

Instantly, everything was in chaos. Sheer panic broke out among the animals in the Beverly Hills section. Lions were roaring and hitting against the sides of their cages; bears were lunging against the bars; chimps were screaming. The water was starting to rock the cages. Some were already floating and were about to be swept downstream.

I didn't know what to do first! I raced for the cages, but was thrown down by the weight of the water. Miguel came running over, yelling half in English and half in Spanish. I told him to grab a large coil of rope that was hanging in a tree nearby. I fastened it around me and, with Miguel holding the other end, I started out into the water. If I could just get to the cages, I could unlock them and set the animals free. At least then they could fend for themselves. It was their only chance. Otherwise, they would all drown in their cages.

The water was rushing past me furiously. I struggled through it to Gentle Ben's cage, fumbling for the key. "For Chrissake, don't *drop* it!" I mumbled to myself. The key turned, I threw open the door, and the great old bear landed right on top of me in his panic for freedom.

I grabbed Ben's heavy coat and hung on as his massive body carried me to a group of cages holding more than twenty animals. The water was now five or six feet deep. Cages were starting to come loose from their foundations; the animals were swimming inside them, fighting for breath. I let go of Ben and grabbed onto the steel bars of one of the cages. My heart sank as I saw Ben dog-paddling, trying to reach the embankment. He never did. I could just barely make out his form as he was carried through some rough white water and around a bend before he was lost from view.

One by one I released the animals—leopards, tigers, bears—talking as calmly as I could, even managing an occasional pat or kiss of farewell. I watched as they were carried away, swept along with the torrent of water. Some would come together for a moment and would then be whisked away, as though a giant hand had come up and shoved them. Some went under. I strained to see whether any of these came up again, but I couldn't tell.

My wonderful, beloved animals were all fighting for their lives. I felt sick and helpless.

To my right, about thirty feet out in the water and half submerged, was a large, heavy steel cage on wheels with a row of four compartments in it. I managed to get to it just as the force of the current started to move it. I began to open the compartments, one by one, but now the cage was moving faster downstream, carrying me with it. I looked back to the shore, at Miguel. He saw the problem, and with his end of the rope he threw a dally around a large tree branch. We were running out of time. If the rope came to the end of its slack before I could get it off me and onto the cage, we would lose the cage. It was picking up speed, and the animals inside were roaring and barking in terror.

I decided to hold the cage myself, with the rope tied around my waist. There were two beautiful wolves in the last cage, Sheba and Rona. Toni and I had raised them since they were pups. I was at their door, fumbling with the lock, when the rope went taut. I thought it would cut me in half. I grabbed the steel bars with both hands, leaving the key in the lock, praying it wouldn't drop out. When I reached down once more to open the lock, the key fell into the water! I was stunned, frozen. I knew I had just signed those animals' death warrants. The water behind the cage was building up a wall of force. I held on as tightly as I could, but finally the cage was ripped out of my hands.

I fell backward into the churning water; when I surfaced, I could see the cage out in the mainstream, racing with the trees, bushes, and sides of buildings, heading on down the raging river. I looked for the last time at Sheba and Rona. They were looking at us quietly as if they knew, but their eyes begged for help. My tears joined the flood as my beloved friends were washed away.

By this time it had become clear to me what had happened. The floodgates on the dam had been opened, all right, but because the ground was already saturated with the thirty inches of rain that had fallen in the last few weeks, it wouldn't absorb any more. At the same time, the new storm had hit, pouring down another fourteen inches in just twenty-four hours. Together, these conditions had caused the flood.

It was a larger flood than any that had been recorded in the area in the last hundred years, and it was made worse because the water had been held up occasionally on its fifteen-mile journey down the canyon by debris in its path. When suddenly released, the water that had built up behind the naturally formed logjams doubled in force. By the time it reached us, huge waves had been built up: the water and debris came crashing down on us like a wall, then subsided, only to come crashing down again. We were to struggle through two days and nights of unbelievable havoc and terror, trying desperately to salvage what we could of the ranch.

The storm grew worse. Heavy sheets of rain filled and overflowed our flood channel, undermining its sides until they caved in. By mid-morning the Santa Clarita had become a raging, murderous torrent, 150 feet wide and 15 feet deep, moving through Africa U.S.A. with the speed and force of an express train. In its fury it wiped out a two-lane highway, full-grown oak trees, generator buildings—everything. Our soundstage was in a full-sized building, 100 feet long by 50 feet wide, but the water just picked it up like a matchbox and carried it away downstream, end over end, rolling it like a toy and depositing it on a sand embankment a mile away. Electric wires flared brightly as the water hit them. We rushed for the main switch to the soundstage, shutting everything down for fear of someone being electrocuted. Everywhere, animals and people were in the water, swimming for safety.

We'd be half drowned, and then we'd make our way to the shore, cough and sputter, and go back into the water. You don't think at a time like that—you *do*. My people risked their lives over and over again for the animals.

The waves next hit the elephant pens, hard. We moved the elephants out as the building collapsed and was carried downstream. Then the waves caught the camels' cage, pulling it into the water. One huge camel was turning over and over as he was swept along. (I thought at the time that somewhere, someday, if that animal drowned, some archeologist would dig up its bones and say, "My God, there must have been camels in Los Angeles!")

We worked frenziedly. Bears, lions, and tigers were jumping out of their cages and immediately being swept downstream. Others were hanging onto our legs and pulling us under, or we were hanging onto them and swimming for shore. I unlocked the cheetah's cage and he sprang out over my head, right into the water, and was gone. Animals were everywhere.

I remember grabbing hold of a mature tiger as he came out of his cage. He carried me on his back to temporary security on the opposite bank as smoothly as if we'd rehearsed it.

Another time I found myself being carried downstream with Zamba, Jr., who was caught in the same whirlpool that I was. I grabbed his mane, and together we swam for the safety of the shore. After resting a bit, I managed to get back to the main area, leaving the lion in as good a spot as any. At least for the moment he was safe.

As the storm rode on, the river was full of animals and people swimming together; there was no "kill" instinct in operation, only that of survival. Men were grabbing fistfuls of fur, clinging for life. A monkey grabbed a lion's tail, which allowed him to make it to safety.

Clarence the cross-eyed lion was in a state of panic. The river had surrounded him and was now flooding his cage. His trainer, Bob, waded across the water, put a chain on Clarence, took him out of his cage, and attempted to jump across the raging stream with him. But the lion wouldn't jump. The water was rising rapidly. Bob threw part of the chain to me. To gain some leverage, I grabbed a pipe that was running alongside a building. As we both pulled, Clarence finally jumped, and just then the pipe I was holding onto came loose. It turned out to be a "hot" electric conduit, for when Clarence leaped and the pipe came loose, we all got a tremendous electric shock! Fortunately, the pipe also pulled the wires loose, so the shock only lasted for an instant. Had it continued, it would certainly have killed us, as we were standing knee-deep in water.

We noticed a group of monkeys trapped in a small outcropping of dirt and debris in the middle of the river. Frank almost died trying to save them: he tied a rope around his waist and started across, but about halfway over he slipped and went under. We didn't know whether to pull on the rope or not. We finally saw him in midstream, trying to stay afloat. Whenever we pulled on the rope, he would go under. (We found out later that the rope had become tangled around his foot, and every time we yanked it we were pulling him under!) But he made it, thank God, and he was able to swim the animals to safety.

We were racing against time. The river was still rising, piling up roots and buildings and pushing them along in front, forming a wall of destruction. The shouts of half-drowned men and the screams of drowning animals filled the air, along with thunder and lightning and the ever-increasing downpour of rain.

Throughout the turmoil and strife one thing was crystal clear to me, and that is that without affection training, all would have been lost. It was extraordinary. As dangerous and frightening as the emergency was, these animals remained calm enough to let themselves be led to safety when it was possible for us to do so.

Imagine yourself in a raging storm, with buildings crashing alongside of you. You make your way to a cage that houses a lion or a tiger, and the animal immediately understands why you're there and is happy to see you. You open the door, put a leash on the animal, and you both jump out into the freezing, swirling water. Together, you're swept down the stream, hitting logs, rolling over and over, as you try to keep your arms around the animal. Together, you get up onto the safety of dry land. You dry off, give your animal a big hug, and then go back in for another one.

There was one big cage left in the back section containing a lion. This lion was a killer who had been fear trained rather than affection trained. We went out to him. The other lions were being saved because we could swim with them, but this fellow was too rough. I got to the cage and opened the door. A couple of my men threw ropes on the lion and pulled, trying to get him out of his potential grave—but he wouldn't come out. He was petrified! We pulled and struggled and fought to get him out of the cage, but we couldn't do it, and we finally had to let him go.

Then the "wild string" panicked, and in their hysteria they attacked their rescuers as if they were enemies. In the end, we had to resort to tranquilizer guns. We fired darts into each fear-trained animal, and as they succumbed to the medication, we held their bodies up above the water and carried them to safety. Tragically, there was not enough time to drag all of them to safety; several drowned in their drugged sleep before we could reach them.

The storm continued on into the night, and with the darkness came a nightmare of confusion. We worked on without sleep, sustained by coffee and desperation.

During that first night, it became clear that ancient Modoc, the elephant, the one-eyed wonder of the big top, had by no means outlived her capacity for calmness and courage in the face of disaster. Modoc took over, understanding fully what was at stake and what was required of her. Animal after animal was saved as she labored at the water's edge, hauling their cages to safety on higher ground. When the current tore a cage free and washed it downstream, Modoc got a firmer grip on the rope with her trunk and, with the power of several bulldozers, steadily dragged the cage back to safety. Then a trainer would attach the rope to another endangered pen, and Modoc would resume her labors.

We eventually became stranded with some of the animals on an island—this was all that was left of Africa U.S.A., plus the area alongside the railroad track. When the dam had burst upstream, the wall of water that hit the ranch divided into two fast-moving rivers. As time passed, the rivers widened and deepened until they were impossible to cross. As dusk fell on the second day, we realized that we were cut off from the mainland.

Since it was the highest ground on the ranch, the island in the center had become the haven for all the survivors. The office building, the vehicles, and about twenty cages were all well above the flooded zone and so were safe for the time being. The giraffes, some monkeys, and one lion were all housed in makeshift cages on the island. We all hoped the water would not rise any further.

Behind the office building ran a railroad track. By following the tracks for three miles, it would be possible to reach the highway. The problem would then be in crossing the torrent of water to get to the road.

I noticed that Bullfrog, our thousand-pound Indian buffalo, was gone. Buffalos are known to be excellent swimmers. Surely *he* could survive! I asked around to see whether anyone had seen him. No one had. Bullfrog's cage had been at the entrance to the ranch, because he always greeted visitors with a most unusual bellow that sounded exactly like the word "Hi." Now he was gone, too. Would it ever end? I felt weak. The temperature had dropped, and the wind had come up. The windchill factor was now thirty degrees below zero.

There's something horrible about tragedy that occurs in the dark. I could hear the water running behind me, and every once in a while I'd hear a big timber go, or an animal cry, or a person shouting. It all seemed very unreal.

Throughout the night and all the next day the rain continued, and we worked on. Luckily, help came from everywhere. The highway, which we could no longer get to but which we could see, was lined with cars. Some people had successfully rigged up a bos'n chair 50 feet in the air and were sending hot food and drink over to us, a distance of some 200 yards. Other people were walking three miles over the hills to bring supplies. Radio communication was set up by a citizens-band club. Gardner McKay, the actor and a true friend, put his Mercedes on the track, deflated the tires, and slowly drove down to help us. One elderly woman prepared ham and coffee and brought it in at two o'clock in the morning, only to find on her return that her car had been broken into and robbed!

Then a train engine came down the track to help (just an engine—no cars). Three girls from the affection-training school volunteered to rescue the snakes. The girls climbed onto the cowcatcher on the front of the engine. We then wrapped about thirty feet of pythons and boa constrictors around their shoulders and told them where to take the snakes once they were on the other side. (There was, of course, no more electricity in the reptile and nursery area, and unless we could get the reptiles to some heat, they would surely die.) Goats, aoudads, and llamas all rode in the coal bin behind the engine. I'll never forget the look on one girl's face as the engine pulled out and a python crawled through her hair.

By four the next morning, some twenty people had, by one method or another, made it over to our island to help. Some chose a dangerous way, tying ropes around their middles and entering the water slowly, with those on the island holding the other ends of the ropes. Then, with the current carrying them quickly downstream, they would look for a logjam or boulder to stop them so they could make their way to where we were.

I was having some coffee in the watchmen's trailer when the scream of an animal shattered the night. I dashed out to find a small group of people huddled together, trying to shine their flashlights on the animal who was out there in the dark, desperately struggling in the raging water. It had succeeded in swimming out of the turbulence in the middle of the stream, but the sides of the river were too slippery for it to get a foothold and climb to safety. In the dark, I couldn't make out which animal it was. Then I heard it: "Hi! Hi!" It was a call of desperation from Bullfrog, the buffalo, as he fought for his life. There was nothing we could do to help him, and his "Hi's" trailed down the dark, black abyss, fading as he was carried away around the bend.

Then Toni screamed at me in the dark, "Ralph, over here!" I fought my way through a maze of debris and water and burst into a clearing. There was Toni, holding a flashlight on—lo and behold—a big steel cage from Beverly Hills! It had been washed downstream and was lodged in the trunk of a toppled tree. It was still upright, but its back was facing us, and we couldn't see inside.

218

We waded out to the cage. Toni kept calling, "Sheba, Rona, are you there? Please answer!" Our hearts were beating fast, and Toni was crying.

Hoping against hope that the wolves were still alive, we rounded the corner, half swimming, half falling. Then we eased up to the front of the cage and looked straight into two sets of the most beautiful eyes I'd ever seen. Rona and Sheba had survived! They practically jumped out of their skins when they saw us, as though to say, "Is it really *you?*" Toni had her key, and we unlocked the door. Both wolves fell all over us, knocking us into the water. They couldn't seem to stop licking our faces and whimpering. Thank God, at least *they* were safe!

The rain finally let up on the morning of the third day. The sun came out, and at last we had time to stop, look around, and assess the damage. It was devastating, and heartrending.

Most of the animals had been let out of their cages and had totally disappeared, including Judy, Clarence, Pajama Tops, the Zebra, and Raunchy, our star jaguar. We knew a few others had definitely drowned. Both rhinos were missing, and so were the hippos. Our beloved Gentle Ben had been washed away, along with hundreds of other animals.

I was sitting there looking at the wreckage when somebody put a cup of hot chocolate in my hand. It was Toni. She stood before me, as exhausted as I was, clothes torn and wet, hair astray, cold and shivering. What a woman! Earlier, she had managed to make her way to the Africa U.S.A. nursery, where all of the baby animals were quartered. Without exception, the babies had all followed her to safety. Not one baby animal had been lost.

The hot liquid felt good going down. I stood up and hugged and kissed Toni, and arm in arm we walked. The sun was just topping the cottonwoods. The river had subsided. All was quiet, except for an occasional animal noise: a yelp, a growl, a snort. All of the animals were happy to see the sun, to feel its warmth.

Toni and I felt only the heavy, leaden feeling of loss. Ten years were, literally, down the drain. We had just signed a contract with Universal Studios to open our beautiful ranch to their tours; this would now be impossible. A million dollars was gone, maybe more. But what was far worse was the loss of some of our beloved animals.

We hiked to a ridge above the railroad track. Something caught my eye, and as we came near an outcrop of trees where we could have a better view, we looked over. There, on top of a nearby hill, we saw an incredible sight. Lying under the tree was Zamba, and at his feet, resting, were a multitude of animals. Deer, bears, tigers, llamas, all lying together peacefully. The animals must have fought their way clear of the treacherous waters and, together, climbed the hill, slept, and then dried off in the morning sun. They hadn't run away. In fact, they seemed to be waiting for our next move. It was as though God had caused the flood to make me realize how powerful affection training is, how deep it had gone. The lamb could truly lie down with the lion, without fear, and could do it by choice!

We called Zam over to us and smothered him with hugs and kisses. As we climbed down to the ranch, the other animals joined us. Camels, giraffes, eland—all came along as we wound our way down.

So many people were there at the ranch! We were once again connected with the rest of the world. Exhausted, wet, wonderful people—true animal lovers. They had come from everywhere. Some were employees, some friends, some strangers. All greeted us as we came down the hill. Their faces expressed hope and love. They cared . . . and it showed.

We took the animals one by one and fed, cleaned, and housed them as best we could.

"Ralph, come quickly!" screamed a voice. "He made it, he made it! *He's alive!*"

"Who, who?" I screamed, and was met by a resounding "Hi, Hi!" From around the corner came Bullfrog—disheveled and muddy, but alive!

"Hi, hi!"

Yes, *hi,* you big, lovable . . . hi! hi!

We began searching for the animals that were still lost. The ranch was a network of people and animals working together on the massive cleanup effort. Animals were straining to pull big trucks out of the water and muck. Bakery trucks were coming by with stale bread for the elephants. Farmers loaned us their skip loaders to round up the hippos and rhinos. (One hippo fell in love with the skip-loader bucket and coyly followed it home!) Charley and Madeline Franks, two loyal helpers, kept hot chili coming and must have dished out hundreds of meals. People from the Humane Society, Fish and Game, Animal Regulation, and the SPCA all helped to comfort and tend the animals.

Everyone was busy constructing makeshift cages. The medical-lab trailer was pulled out of the mud. The nursery building and all of its kitchen storage area had been completely submerged, and some of it had been washed away. However, what could be salvaged was taken up to the island for immediate use.

Outside the ranch, the animals began turning up everywhere. Elephants showed up in people's backyards. Eagles sat in the limbs of trees. Llamas and guanacos cruised the local restaurants and were seen in parking lots. There was no difficulty between animals and people.

We had had dozens of alligators, some weighing two hundred to three hundred pounds. The whole pen had been hit by the water; we lost most of them because the water was ice-cold, and it battered and beat them. For seven months afterward we'd read in the paper that the bodies of alligators were being found everywhere, up to forty-five miles away. There were helicopter and airplane photos of alligators that had been killed, their bodies lying in the sand as the water subsided.

Of 1500 other animals, only 9 had drowned. Five of these were animals that had not been affection trained.

Only one animal remained lost and unaccounted for, and that was old Gentle Ben. I had last seen him being swept sideways down the river. We didn't have much hope for him.

I was starting to feel the full shock of everything that had happened. True, by some miracle most of the animals were safe, but other losses had been enormous. As the emergency lessened and mopping-up operations took over, I felt worse and worse. The shakes set in, and then I developed a high fever. The doctors said it was a walking pneumonia, and that rest, good food, and warmth were in order. But there were still too many things to do—now was not the time to stop. I did, however, need to find a place to sit down and relax for a while.

As I sat on a log, my body trembled with shock as well as illness. In looking over the debris, it seemed to me that everything I had worked for was gone. The emotional pain, the sheer physical exhaustion, and the pneumonia had overloaded me. I just couldn't handle any more. I had no more tears, no pain of any kind. I was numb. I sat in the middle of the chaos with an old blanket wrapped around me, unmoving, unable to give any more orders.

I had closed my eyes and was drifting off to sleep when something warm and wet on my face woke me up. I opened my eyes and saw Ben. *Gentle Ben had come home!!* I hugged him and cried like a big kid. I turned to get up to tell everyone, but I didn't have to. They were all there. Toni, joined by the rest, had brought him to me. He'd been found two miles down the canyon, mud-covered and a few pounds lighter, but safe! Tears were in everybody's eyes—and if you looked closely, it seemed that even old Ben had a few.

A beautiful rainbow arched its brilliant colors across the ravaged countryside, then was gone.

✻

There was a time in my life when I felt I had reached the end of the rainbow. I had touched it, had dug my hand deep into its treasures of happiness and prosperity.

Suddenly, everything had changed. All that I had created was gone. I hadn't realized how vulnerable the world is, how delicate the balance of forces that sustain our existence.

I stood up and dusted off my jeans. In the distance I could see the sky clearing, and I knew that some day there would be another rainbow, its treasure awaiting. Until then, we had a job to do. We would need to start all over again.

EPILOGUE

Imagine yourself in a foreign country, where you speak not a word of the language, know nothing of the customs, and are of a different race than the indigenous people. How you would long to feel accepted by the inhabitants, to be welcomed by them in their homes and hearts.

So it was with me and the animals. For many years I stood on the outside of their world, longing to enter, to speak their language, to learn their ways.

How fortunate I am that they finally showed me the secret door through which I could enter their kingdom!

To the animals, I say thank you. Thank you for letting me into your world, for giving me the thrill of riding a giraffe, picnicking with a gorilla, swimming with an elephant, wrestling a tiger, and riding a rhino.

Thank you for teaching me that instinct is God's voice. *While people read from the Bible, animals talk with its author.*

Nature is perfect, though man is not. It is man who has taken your land, eaten your flesh, hunted for your skins. I am deeply sorry that man has missed the wonder that you are.

For millions of years, you were the caretakers of the earth. Now man has that responsibility.

While we still have a chance, let us learn to respect the beauty of the beasts.